501
HINTS & TIPS
WITH
VINEGAR

igloobooks

Published in 2014
by Igloo Books Ltd
Cottage Farm
Sywell
NN6 0BJ
www.igloobooks.com

FIR003 0614
2 4 6 8 10 9 7 5 3
ISBN 978-1-78197-392-9

Images copyright Thinkstock/Getty Images

Printed and manufactured in China

Publisher's Note:
The reader is advised not to regard the medical
suggestions and techniques described in this book as
substitutes for the advice of a qualified medical practitioner.
The reader follows the ideas in this book solely at his or her own risk.

contents

Introduction

Vinegar is one of those household staples that we all have in our kitchen cabinet. It is thought to have been discovered when a cask of wine was left and allowed to go off, which is how we get the word vinegar (from the French *vin aigre*, or sour wine).

The basic process behind making vinegar is the fermentation of carbohydrates and sugars in order to produce ethanol, which is a type of alcohol, and then a secondary fermentation of the ethanol to produce acetic acid. This is why wine that is past its best really does taste like something you should be using to pickle with!

The culinary and medicinal uses of vinegar have been documented throughout history. It is mentioned in the Bible and traces have been found in Egyptian urns. Hippocrates (c. 460–370 B.C.), the father of modern medicine, recognized its antibacterial qualities. The Greeks used it as a food preservative and recommended it as a remedy for many different ailments, including coughs and congestion.

Roman soldiers drank diluted vinegar as a tonic, while Roman ladies relied on it as an ingredient in their cosmetics. Before the development of chemically laden cleaning products, people used to turn to vinegar. It seems to have fallen out of touch as a cleaning agent in the last generation or two, although many of us have vague memories of our grandmothers using it around the home, if only for cleaning windows.

Interest has been re-awakened, however, as a greater awareness of the harm we might be doing to our planet leads us to seek more natural products. Vinegar also appeals to the thrifty among us. Why pay over the odds for costly products when we can do so many of the same jobs far less expensively?

Virtues of Vinegar

If you are unsure of the benefits of using vinegar as part of your usual domestic routine or to help you with household chores, then consider the following interesting points:

good for you

You don't have to worry about handling vinegar. Not only is it an entirely natural product, it also helps to regulate the pH levels of your skin, and can be used as a skin tonic.

good for the planet

All the chemicals we use to clean our homes get washed down our drains and into the water table or the sea, which has a detrimental effect on our ecosystem. Vinegar is biodegradable and will not cause any harm.

good for your bank balance

Throw a few cleaning products into your shopping trolley and you soon see how your weekly shopping bill shoots up. But white distilled vinegar will do just as good a job as any of those more expensive products at a fraction of the cost.

Types of Vinegar

If you look on your supermarket shelf, you'll find a huge variety of different vinegars on offer, from the standard brown malt to a number of unique ones produced to appeal to the connoisseur food market. Some are better for cleaning, some for health, others for use in your preferred recipes. The basic ingredient used for the fermentation process dictates the final flavor and quality.

White Distilled Vinegar

This clear liquid is high in acidity and so is good for cleaning. Buy it in as large a quantity as you can find to reap the greatest cost benefits. Not to be confused with white wine vinegar, which is more expensive to buy, and better used in cooking.

White Spirit Vinegar

This is harder to get hold of than white distilled vinegar. Brewed from molasses, it has a less pungent smell.

Malt Vinegar

Brown in color, this basic vinegar with a robust, distinctive taste is made from malted barley rather than wine. Beloved by the British for sprinkling on French fries, it is mostly used for pickling.

Wine Vinegar

Available in red and white varieties, or even specific grape varieties such as Champagne, wine vinegar is less acidic than cider or white vinegar and is a popular cooking ingredient.

Balsamic Vinegar

The favorite of all foodies, this has become a bit of a cliché ingredient in recent years. Originally brewed in Modena, Italy, from pressings of the Trebbiano grape, it is traditionally aged over many years in oak casks. Dark brown in color, it has a rich, sweet flavor so intense that only a small amount is needed to impart taste.

Japanese Rice Vinegar

Mild in flavor, and typically only containing 5% acetic acid, rice vinegar is pale to almost colorless in appearance and is a popular ingredient in sushi. As the name suggests, it is made from fermented rice, though a stronger-tasting variety called 'seasoned rice vinegar' is made from sake.

Apple Cider Vinegar

Apple cider vinegar has an unparalleled reputation as a health tonic; aficionados swear by its health-giving qualities, though the evidence is anecdotal.

Fruit Vinegar

Fruit vinegars can either be brewed from specific, single fruits – raspberry is a very common one – or they can be made by adding fruit to white wine vinegar or cider vinegar.

1
general household

If you've previously only regarded vinegar as a cooking ingredient, good for dressing salads or pickling, you will be amazed what you can achieve with a humble bottle of vinegar in your cleaning arsenal.

The best type of vinegar to use for any cleaning task is always white distilled vinegar. It is less pungent than the malt brown vinegar it is distilled from, but still acidic enough to be effective. Don't confuse it with pickling vinegar, which also looks clear and is sold in large jars. Pickling vinegar usually has added spices and flavourings, which you don't want or need when you are cleaning, and is more expensive to buy in any case.

When you discover just how versatile vinegar is, you will soon be using lots of it. Buy the biggest bottles you can find in your supermarket, or order catering-sized bottles online.

make your own cleaning products

Do you have a cupboard crammed with cleaning products, each one designed to do a specific job? Do you have an anti-bacterial spray for your kitchen surfaces, another for your oven, one to remove limescale, and something scary-looking for the toilet? Well, banish them all, and replace them with just one key ingredient that you mix with a few other store cupboard staples: white distilled vinegar.

1 Make furniture polish by combining 3 parts olive oil with 1 part white vinegar and apply with a soft cloth. This does not keep because of the olive oil content, so make up small quantities as you need to use it.

2 You can add a few drops of an essential oil such as lavender or vanilla if you want to add scent to the room at the same time.

3 For tougher surfaces, make a paste that you can use as a scrubbing agent – mix white vinegar with a coarse grained salt.

4 For a general spray for cleaning down kitchen surfaces, mix a 50:50 solution of white distilled vinegar and water, and keep the bottle under the sink. Keep another bottle with undiluted vinegar for tougher jobs - just make sure you label them clearly.

5 Make a scouring cleanser to use on worktops by combining 2 parts of baking soda to 1 part liquid detergent. Then add a teaspoon of white distilled vinegar and mix to form a creamy texture.

spray away

Buy cheap plastic spray bottles from garden centers or, better still, recycle your old ones from other cleaning products you no longer need to use. Just make sure you clean them out thoroughly with plenty of clean water.

everyday surfaces

Floors and walls pick up all sort of dirt, on floors it's tracked in on our shoes and they need regular cleaning. Vinegar is good for your hands so there is no need to wear rubber gloves when scrubbing – a Mrs Mop headscarf is entirely a matter of personal choice. And don't ignore your walls. Over time they attract a greasy film, especially in kitchens.

1 Wooden floors can develop a greasy layer that's hard to shift. Add a cup of white distilled vinegar to very hot water, and make sure you wring out the mop well, as too much water sloshing around will damage the wood.

2 When mopping vinyl or laminate flooring add a cup of white distilled vinegar to the mop bucket of hot water to cut through grime.

3 Keep ceramic floor tiles sparking by adding white distilled vinegar to the cleaning water.

4 If you've moved into a house with greasy, nicotine-stained walls, use a stronger solution of half vinegar and half warm water to restore them to their former glory – or to prepare them for painting.

5 Remove smoke stains on walls from wood fires or candles with a 50:50 solution of white vinegar and water. Spray on and wipe off.

6 Mildew can develop on walls in areas that are poorly ventilated. Wash down with a 50:50 solution of vinegar and hot water. If the problem persists mist the area with neat vinegar and allow to dry. The vinegar will help prevent further build-up.

7 To keep wall tiles gleaming, mix 1 part white distilled vinegar to 3 parts water and use a cloth to wipe the tiles clean. This can also help to preserve the color of the grout.

8 Disinfect and clean your work surfaces by wiping them with neat white distilled vinegar.

help, I'm melting . . .

Do not use vinegar on marble or limestone, whether worktops or floors. The calcium carbonate content will react with the acid in vinegar and start to dissolve.

sparkly windows and mirrors

We've all been there. You take on the back-breaking job of washing the windows, sit back and congratulate yourself, only for the sun to come out and reveal all of those dried-on streaks. As generations of women have known, when it comes to all types of glassware, you need to reach for the vinegar bottle.

1 For windows, the best recipe is 3 parts water (as hot as you can stand on your hands) to 1 part white vinegar, with just a small squirt of dish-washing liquid.

2 If you've been using commercial products on your windows, they've probably left a residue. It might take a couple of sessions with your vinegar mix to remove this, so persevere.

3 Always tackle the inside and outside of windows separately. The outside ones are much dirtier and you will need to change your washing liquid and cloth much more frequently.

4 If you really want to channel your grandmother, finish off with some scrunched-up newspaper for a final polish.

5 For drinking glasses and tumblers that have gone cloudy, submerge in warmed vinegar for an hour, then rinse and clean thoroughly.

6 Pour 1 to 2 cups of white vinegar in the bottom of your dishwasher with the usual detergent. Run for a full cycle, and marvel at your extra sparkly glassware.

7 To clean smears from photo frames, wipe using a cloth with a solution of 1 tablespoon of white distilled vinegar and 3 tablespoons of water.

8 To clear fingerprints from your mobile phone screen, mix 1 tablespoon of white distilled vinegar and 1 cup of water, dip a cloth in it and wipe clean.

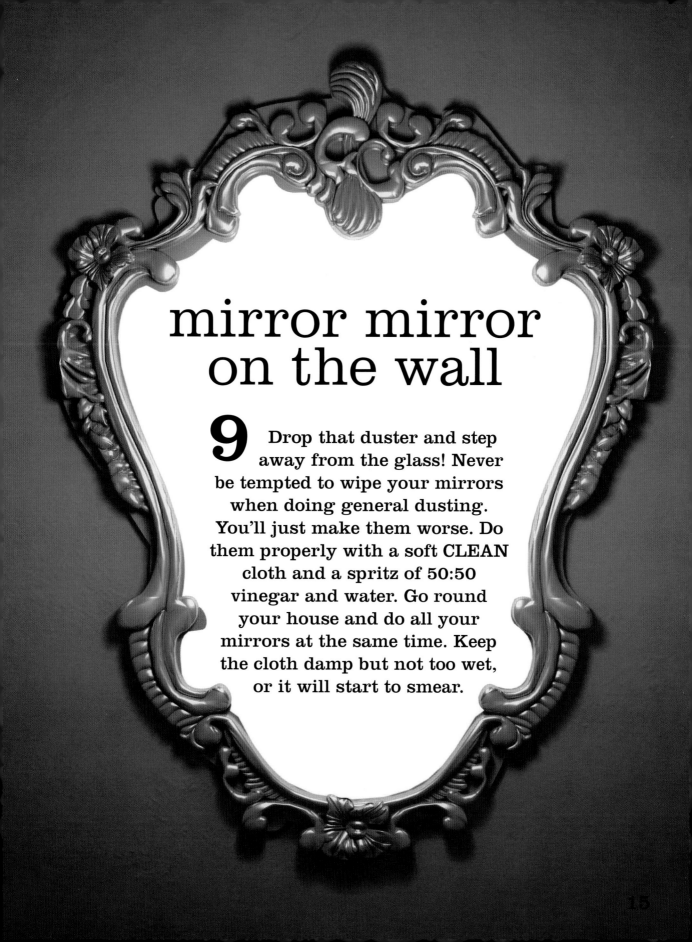

mirror mirror on the wall

9 Drop that duster and step away from the glass! Never be tempted to wipe your mirrors when doing general dusting. You'll just make them worse. Do them properly with a soft CLEAN cloth and a spritz of 50:50 vinegar and water. Go round your house and do all your mirrors at the same time. Keep the cloth damp but not too wet, or it will start to smear.

remove that whiff!

There's nothing more embarrassing than being aware of an odour around your home, especially when you have guests. You might think of vinegar as being a stinky substance itself, but did you know it can actually help to remove and neutralize unwanted smells, whether from cooking, pets or cigarettes?

1 If you have been cooking something smelly in the kitchen, such as fish or curry, boil a pan of water with a cup of vinegar added on the hob to quickly clear the pong.

2 If you keep a bin for food scraps to recycle or to add to your compost heap, this can soon turn nasally challenging. When you empty it, wash thoroughly and then wipe out with neat vinegar and allow to dry. The remaining residue will help counteract stinky smells but won't have any detrimental effect on the food to be recycled.

3 Plastic lunch boxes can absorb the smell of their contents, which does not disappear with ordinary washing. Wipe out with neat white vinegar and allow to dry thoroughly to shift the lingering smell.

4 For a natural air freshener that won't pump nasty chemicals around your home, place saucers of neat vinegar in unobtrusive places.

5 If sinks and garbage disposal units begin to emit unwelcome smells, especially in warmer weather, pour a glug of neat vinegar down the plughole last thing before you go to bed, and leave overnight.

6 Keep a spray bottle filled with neat white distilled vinegar and just spritz in the air when you encounter bad smells. The vinegar whiff will quickly go, and the bad smell along with it. If you like, you can add a few drops of essential oil, such as lavender or vanilla.

banish those wash day blues

Ah, the lovely washing machine. This has to be the single most useful piece of kit in our homes. Now doesn't that machine deserve the best care you can give it? Well, how about a vinegar spa treatment?

1 Does your machine give off a pong when you open the door? Pour 2 to 3 cups of white distilled vinegar into the base of the machine, and then run the machine empty on the hottest wash it can do. Repeat every 4 to 6 weeks.

2 If you use liquid detergent, the dispenser can become clogged and greasy. Pour neat vinegar into the dispenser when you do your hot wash to give it a thorough clean.

3 To aid thorough rinsing of clothes, add a cup of vinegar to the rinse cycle (use the dispenser for adding fabric softener).

4 Vinegar is a natural brightener, both of colored and white fabrics. Adding a cup of vinegar to the wash will brighten colors and whiten whites.

5 To prevent brightly colored new clothes from running, soak them in vinegar for 10 minutes before adding them to the wash load. The vinegar acts as a dye fixative.

6 Washed a paper tissue by mistake? Remove as much as you can by hand and then re-run the load with a cup of vinegar added to remove the smaller bits.

7 It can be tricky to clean out awkward corners on the filter on your tumble drier. Soak overnight in neat vinegar and then rinse thoroughly.

8 Woollen and cotton blankets fluff up beautifully if you add a cup of vinegar to the rinse cycle.

11 To wash fabric handkerchiefs, soak them in a 50:50 vinegar solution before the main wash. This will kill germs and keep them looking bright.

12 Fabric conditioners are very expensive, instead, add a cup of white distilled vinegar to your rinse cycle to keep your linen soft.

13 To reduce static in clothes, add a cup of white distilled vinegar to your rinse cycle.

14 Reduce the amount of lint on your clothes by adding a cup of white distlled vinegar to your rinse cycle.

9 Delicate wool cycles are ineffective at removing perspiration smells. Add vinegar to the main wash. If smells persist, soak in 50:50 vinegar water solution for 10 minutes and rinse.

15 Remove soap residue from black clothes by adding a cup of white distilled vinegar to your final rinse.

10 Cuff and collar stains will age a shirt long before the rest of it has given up. Treat those areas by rubbing in a paste of equal parts baking soda and vinegar before washing as usual.

16 If you've left your clothes in the washing machine too long, pour a cup of white distilled vinegar into the machine and wash in hot water. Then repeat your wash using detergent.

steam away smoke

Cigarette smoke is less of a problem these days, now that it is banned in most public areas. But if you have been unlucky enough to have been caught in the backdraft of a nicotine-addicted friend, you will want to remove that nose-wrinkling pong from your clothes as soon as possible.

1 A steam treatment works wonders. Fill a bathtub with very hot water and 3 or 4 cupfuls of vinegar. Suspend the item of clothing, on a hanger, above the steam until the water cools naturally. Pong be gone!

2 If you're more of an outdoors person, the above treatment works just as well to remove wood smoke or barbecue smells from jumpers, coats and jackets that you don't want to put in the washing machine.

3 To get rid of lingering smoke whiffs, place a shallow bowl filled with white distilled vinegar in the centre of the room.

4 Remove nicotine stains and whiffs from your fingers by rubbing them with neat, white distilled vinegar.

5 To remove light scorch marks from fabrics, rub with white distilled vinegar and wipe with a dry cloth.

a pressing matter

There is nothing better than putting on some beautifully ironed clothes to make you feel great. But your ironing skills will only be as good as the equipment you use, so it is important to keep your iron in tip-top condition. A common problem is that your iron may not be letting off steam like it used to. This could be because scale deposits have built up in the vent holes.

1 To clear them, pour a mix of equal parts water and white wine vinegar into the reservoir until it is full. Set the iron to its highest steam setting (or use the cleaning function if it has one) and allow the vinegar steam to spew forth for a few minutes. Watch out – it will be spitting out hot bits. When the steam has finished, iron an old dish towel for a few minutes to clear out any lingering muck.

2 For a final flourish, allow the iron to cool completely and then scrub the base plate with a paste of equal parts salt and white vinegar. Wipe with a clean cloth dipped in vinegar and any scorch marks will disappear. Iron your trusty dish towel once more to remove any residue.

3 Don't forget the ironing board cover. A deep steam treatment will perk it up in no time. Spray the whole cover with a 50:50 mix of white vinegar and water, and then iron dry to release the vinegary steam through the fabric.

4 To create sharp creases in clothes, lightly spray them with equal parts vinegar and water before ironing.

120Vac 60Hz 1200W
DO NOT IMMERSE - NE PAS IMMERGER
MADE IN CHINA-FABRIQUE EN CHINE

nightmare stains

Been a bit clumsy? Don't worry, vinegar will come to your rescue and banish those blemishes. But remember to use white distilled vinegar: red wine vinegar, malt vinegar and balsamic vinegar will all cause a stain themselves, so don't go splashing those around or you'll just make things worse!

1 For tomato, tea, coffee, mustard, cosmetics and fruit stains, spray with neat vinegar until soaked then wash as usual. Repeat the process as necessary for stubborn marks.

2 For wine and grease, treat the stain as soon as you can for best results. Flood the stained area with undiluted white vinegar and wash immediately. For older stains soak the article overnight in a bowl of water with a cup of vinegar added, then wash.

3 Some stains present a real challenge to shift. For ink, mix 1 part vinegar to 1 part cornstarch and apply this paste to the area. Leave to dry, then wash as normal.

4 Stains under the arms of clothes are a mix of sweat and antiperspirant. Spray with vinegar, then rub with sea salt or any other coarse-grained salt. Allow to dry before washing. Placing the item in the sun as it dries helps.

5 Mildew stains are tricky and often resist a normal wash cycle, especially at low temperatures. But they respond well to vinegar because of its antibacterial qualities. Pre-treat the area by spraying it with undiluted white vinegar and then leaving it for 10 minutes.

6 Remove crayon marks the easy way by dipping an old toothbrush in white distilled vinegar and gently rubbing the area affected.

Oops!

7 Vinegar can damage some silks, acetates or rayons. When using undiluted vinegar on delicate fabrics, always test on a hidden seam allowance first.

8 Heat will set protein stains, such as blood, egg and milk, so always soak in cold water with a cup of vinegar, rather than hot water.

fresher carpets, curtains and rugs

Comforting and cocooning or a bit whiffy and grubby looking, how are your soft furnishings? Fabrics in the home absorb smells over time and pick up dirt and grease from daily contact. Whizz through your home with your trusty vinegar to hand to refresh and renew. Everything will smell sweet and your home will thank you for it.

1 Treat marks on carpets and rugs by lightly spraying with vinegar – do not soak the area, just dampen. Sprinkle with baking soda and allow to dry. Vacuum up the remains. Test on an area normally covered by furniture first.

2 Many curtains are dry clean only, but you can freshen them up inbetween cleans with a vinegar mist. Keep the solution fairly weak – about 1 part vinegar to 9 parts water. Use a spray bottle with adjustable settings (you can buy these in a garden center) and use the finest mist setting. Test a hidden section first, then if you are happy with the result, spray all over on both sides. Keep the curtains closed while they dry.

3 Use the same refreshing spray on your upholstered sofas and chairs. Again, try a hidden test patch first to make sure there is no damage to your fabric. It's best to do this on a sunny day to speed up the drying process. Make sure you don't overwet any area.

4 To brighten lace curtains, hand wash them in a bathtub filled with lukewarm water, a small amount of detergent designed for delicate fabrics and a cup of white vinegar.

5 For an extra level of cleanliness use vinegar instead of fabric softener when washing your sheets and bedding. This is a great tip if anyone in the family has allergies.

6 Urine stains on mattresses – not the topic of polite conversation perhaps, but an annoying fact of life. Wash the area as soon as possible with cold water and a small amount of your usual liquid or powder laundry detergent. Then rinse with a solution of cold water with a cup of vinegar added. Allow to dry thoroughly, for at least 24 hours if possible.

7 When you take your curtains down, take the chance to clean the metal rings to remove any rust patches that can stain your curtains, and restore sheen. Place them in a metal saucepan, cover with white vinegar and heat gently until the vinegar is warm. Turn off the heat and allow them to stand for half an hour. Rinse with clean water, then dry thoroughly.

8 To brighten the color of your carpet, mix a solution of 1 cup of vinegar to 1 gallon of water. Then brush this into the carpet and leave to dry out naturally.

9 To clean leather sofas and chairs mix a 50:50 solution of white distilled vinegar and linseed oil. Spray the solution on to them and wipe clean with a damp cloth.

plumbing the depths

Sinks, faucets (taps), and drains really are grime magnets.
Hard water, food grease in kitchens, soap scum,
limescale, hair, toothpaste – sounds like a really revolting
recipe, doesn't it? To keep your cleaning zones, well,
clean, bring on the vinegar. It will do an amazing job
clearing through grease and dirt, without polluting our
waterways.

1 Scrub as much as you like, clearing around the base of faucets (taps) has to be one of the trickiest jobs. Well, try it the easy way. Soak an old cotton rag in undiluted white vinegar and wrap it tightly around the base. Leave overnight, and the grime will lift easily with the help of an old toothbrush.

2 To clean around the plug hole, put the plug in and pour in enough vinegar to completely cover. Leave overnight, then drain and wipe clean with a cloth.

3 The underside of plugs can look rather too much like petri dishes for comfort. Soak them in a glass jar of vinegar overnight to remove slime and grime. For those that are attached, place the jar in the sink itself.

4 Give the whole sink a soak to remove that stubborn film of grease and scale. Fill completely with equal part vinegar and hot water and leave overnight.

5 To clean the overflow, use a spray bottle to spray lots of undiluted vinegar into the hole, and then allow it to drip down and do its work.

6 Do you have scale build-up at the end of your faucet (tap) spout? Fill a plastic cup full of vinegar, place it round the end of the faucet and then fix it in place with either masking tape or by tying a dish towel round it. Leave overnight, then wipe clean the next day.

clearing a blockage

Problems in your pipework? The first sign can be that sinks are slow to empty. If this is the case, or you have a full-scale blockage, try a little home chemistry.

1 First pour 2 cups of baking soda, then 1 cup of white vinegar, down the plug hole. When it has stopped fizzing, empty a whole kettle of boiling water down the drain. Repeat until the sink drains freely.

2 To keep it that way, apply a weekly dose of a tablespoon of baking soda and a cupful of vinegar.

3 To make your drains smell better, pour 1 cup of baking soda and 1 cup of white distilled vinegar down the drain. Leave for 10 minutes and then let the hot water run for 1 minute.

usehold

beautiful baths

It stands to reason that if we are going to keep ourselves clean, we need to make sure the place we go to get clean stays clean. Logical, isn't it? Vinegar is a wonderful bathroom cleaner – both efficient and hygienic. Just a word of warning if you have marble tiles or fittings: marble and vinegar DO NOT mix, as the acid disintegrates the surface.

1 Run your fingers along the surface of ceramic or stone tiles and you can feel a grimy layer. To cut through this, use a paste of equal parts vinegar, baking soda, and salt, applied with a non-abrasive sponge. Rinse clean afterwards with some water.

2 Mildew build-up on the grout between tiles is notoriously difficult to remove. Spray generously with neat white distilled vinegar and allow to soak in for at least an hour. Scrub clean with a toothbrush and cold water, and rinse away. To stop it creeping back again, spray dry grout once a month with a 50:50 solution of white wine vinegar and allow to dry.

3 If you have a stubborn mark around the bath, use an old nailbrush to apply your tile-cleaning paste and remove the ring.

4 Dripping taps can leave unsightly brown stains, especially on older or antique bathtubs and hand basins. Use the same super paste to treat those.

5 Plastic or rubber bath mats are great to prevent slipping, especially if you have your shower over the tub, but boy can they habor dirt. Spray the underside with undiluted vinegar to clear any mildew or slimy stuff, leave the vinegar to work its magic for a couple of hours, then blast with clean water from the shower.

6 To shine the chrome fixtures in your bathroom, apply neat vinegar and buff them using a cloth to make them gleam.

7 To keep your sponges fresh and avoid product build-up, soak them in neat white distilled vinegar overnight. Rinse the next day in cold water and allow to dry naturally.

revolting shower curtains

If you spend your whole shower doing a complicated dance to make sure no part of you touches the shower curtain because it's just too disgusting, it's time to take action.

1 To keep your shower curtains clean and fresh, wash at least once a month in the washing machine, adding a cupful of vinegar with your usual detergent. Remove from the washing machine as soon as the cycle has finished and hang up on the shower rail opened out until it is completely dry.

2 If your curtain isn't machine washable, soak it in the bathtub with a cupful of vinegar added, then rinse thoroughly and dry as before.

3 Shift stubborn black mildew or orange soap scum stains along the bottom hem of your curtain by spraying with neat white wine vinegar and scrubbing with an old nailbrush.

sparkling showers

Did you know that when you're happily warbling in the shower scrubbing your back you're actually depositing a fine spray of soap scum and body fat all around you? If that thought is enough to stop you mid-song, don't worry. You can soon restore your shower to pristine freshness with a few vinegar tricks.

1 In those hard-to-reach corners where soap scum and limescale build up, soak an old cotton rag in neat vinegar, push it right into the corner and leave overnight. Remove the loosened dirt with a toothbrush in the morning.

2 In hard water areas, the calcium carbonate (or limescale) builds up and eventually closes up the holes on a shower head, resulting in poorer flow and annoying sideways spray. Unscrew plastic and chrome heads and leave them overnight in a plastic bowl filled with neat white distilled vinegar to shift scaly deposits and restore full water force.

3 If you have a fixed shower head, fill a plastic bag with white distilled vinegar and tape it over the shower head. Let it soak overnight, remove the bag and wipe clean.

4 If you have a glass shower screen, keep it streak-free by cleaning it with scrunched up newspaper soaked in vinegar. Do not rinse afterwards – the fine layer of vinegar left on the glass will help repel dirt.

5 Shower door runners are tricky to clean and harbor dirt. If you can, fill them with neat vinegar and leave to soak for 10 minutes to shift deposits. If they won't hold liquid, use a toothbrush or a cotton tip soaked in neat vinegar to clear out hard-to-reach goo.

6 If you have separate shower tray, put in the plug and fill the whole thing with equal parts vinegar and hot water, and leave overnight. Simply wipe out the following day.

bathrooms

tackle the toilet

Conditioned by years of scary advertising, when it comes to the toilet many people feel compelled to go in with all guns blazing on the chemical front. There really is no need. Vinegar is a natural anti-bacterial agent without the nasties.

1 Pour a cup or two of vinegar into the bowl and allow to sit for an hour or two, before cleaning as usual.

2 Use a spray gun filled with undiluted vinegar to aim right under the rim.

3 To keep your toilet brush germ-free, fill the container with equal parts water and vinegar and leave overnight. Keep a small amount of undiluted vinegar in the base of the toilet brush holder so that it stays that way.

4 To keep your cistern clear, remove the lid, flush the toilet, and add a cup of vinegar to the cistern as it fills.

5 Pour 2 cups of white distilled vinegar into the toilet bowl and leave for 1 hour, to eliminate bad smells.

6 To make your toilet bowl gleam, pour a solution of 1 cup of white distilled vinegar and 1 cup of water into the bowl and leave overnight. The next day, scrub it using a clean toilet brush and flush.

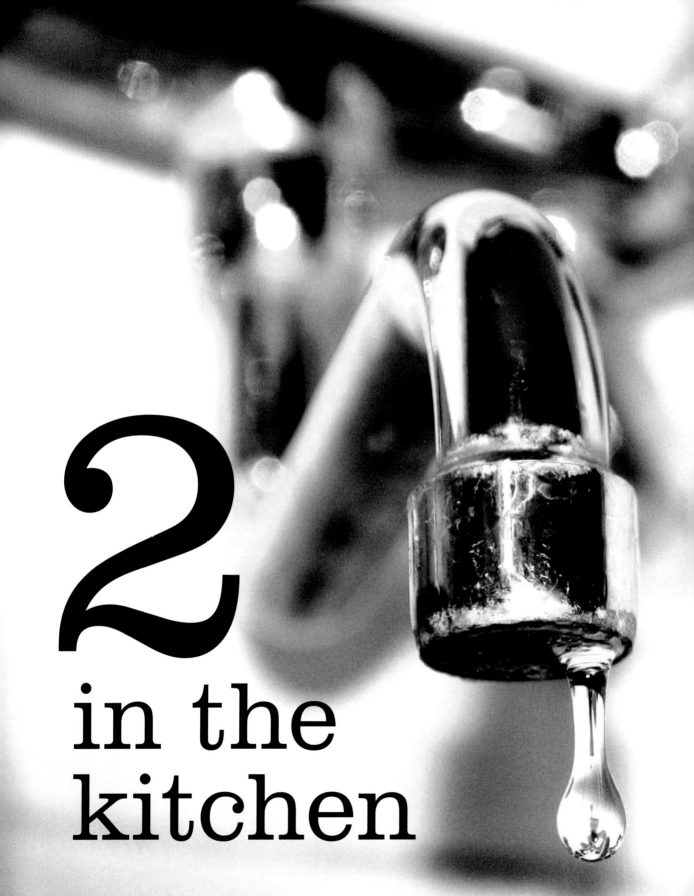

2
in the kitchen

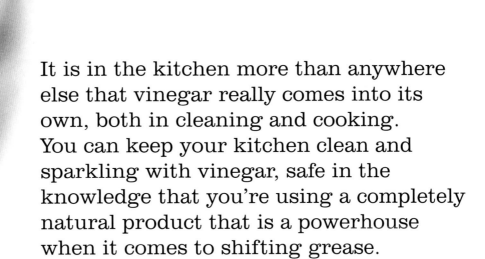

It is in the kitchen more than anywhere else that vinegar really comes into its own, both in cleaning and cooking. You can keep your kitchen clean and sparkling with vinegar, safe in the knowledge that you're using a completely natural product that is a powerhouse when it comes to shifting grease.

Vinegar has proved itself to be incredibly versatile in cooking – it can even be used in baking. Take some time to explore the varieties vinegar comes in, as well as their many different culinary uses. From the essential balsamic vinegar, which no self-respecting modern cook would admit to being without, to the culinary workhorses red and white wine vinegar, and even the humble malt vinegar, there is a recipe that vinegar can help you with. You can even learn how to make wonderful tasty vinegars, which are a great standby when you are making sauces and dressings. They also make fantastic gifts when presented in an attractive bottle with a pretty label.

kitchen equipment and appliances

Vinegar is the perfect cleaning agent for the kitchen because it won't taint food. No one likes the soapy taste that you get from the residual effects of harsh chemical sprays. And, if you've been brainwashed by all those adverts about killer bugs lurking on every surface, you can rest easy at night – vinegar is a natural antibacterial agent.

1 Change cloths regularly, ideally every day, and wash them in a washing machine with some vinegar added to the final rinse.

2 To get sponges and plastic brushes really clean, soak them overnight in neat vinegar.

3 Soak teaspoons in neat vinegar overnight, and scour the insides of mugs with equal quantities of salt and vinegar mixed into a paste.

4 Keep a spray bottle of a 50:50 vinegar and water mix under your sink, and use this as an everyday cleaner to wipe down countertops, the drainer and your sink. This will clean existing dirt, help repel grease and also kill germs. Won't you feel virtuous!

5 If you need to remove stubborn stains, such as red wine or curry spices – turmeric is the worst – from a worktop, make a paste of equal parts baking soda and white wine vinegar, and rub it into the surface well before wiping away.

6 The plastic trays on vegetable steamers can get stained with steam – especially if you cook a lot of carrots. Soak the trays in a 50:50 solution of vinegar and water, and then add a tablespoon of vinegar to the water reservoir every time you steam.

7 Wooden chopping boards can hold germs. Clean and disinfect them by wiping them down with your diluted vinegar spray.

8 To keep garbage disposal units running cleanly, make a tray full of vinegar ice cubes, using equal amounts of water and vinegar, and then let the unit chomp them up.

9 Bread boxes can develop a smell of bread that's just about to turn green. If this is the case, wipe out all crumbs and debris, and wipe down with your diluted worktop spray. Then, soak a piece of bread in neat vinegar and leave it in there overnight to clear the smell.

10 Remove spots on stainless steel or aluminium kitchen pots and pans by rubbing them with neat white distilled vinegar.

11 Make your aluminium kitchen utensils shine by soaking them in a bowl of 1 litre of boiling water and 2 tablespoons of white distilled vinegar. Once cooled, remove each utensil and buff using a tea towel.

12 When rinsing the dishes, use white distilled vinegar and water to rinse. This will leave them squeaky clean and prevent water marks.

13 Keep your tin opener clean and free from rust by scrubbing it with neat vinegar and an old toothbrush.

14 To help your washing-up liquid last longer and also increase the antibacterial quality, add 3 tablespoons of white distilled vinegar tot eh bottle and shake vigorously.

15 Clean your counter tops using a cloth and neat white distilled vinegar to make them smell fresh and rid bacteria.

16 Pour ½ cup of hot white distilled vinegar and ½ cup of baking soda down the garbage disposal, to keep it smelling fresh. Let it sit for a few minutes and then run the hot water to drain it away.

17 Dampen a cloth with white distilled vinegar and wipe out plastic food containers. This will help remove stains and also keep them smelling nice.

18 If your lunch box has taken on a musty smell, then place a slice of bread that has been soaked in vinegar inside it and leave it overnight to soak up the bad smells.

cleaning

scale away

Kitchen appliances are our friends, there's no denying it. But if you live in a hard-water area, you have to give those gadgets a lot of tender loving care to keep them in tip-top condition. If you let scale build up, the machines just can't give of their best. And you're the one who will suffer.

acid attack

Scale is basically the build-up of deposits of the calcium carbonate found in hard water and left behind as it dries. The calcium will dissolve in acid, so vinegar is the ideal liquid to use because it won't damage the machines themselves.

1 No one likes that feeling of draining the dregs of a nice cup of coffee and getting a gritty taste in the mouth. Yes, it's time to de-scale the coffee maker. Fill the reservoir about a third full with vinegar, then top up with water to the fill level, and turn the machine on (without any coffee added, obviously). Run through a second time with clean water only.

2 If you've reached the stage when you can predict the future by reading the scale patterns in the bottom of your teacup, then you might want to check out your kettle. If it's really scaled up, fill the bottom third with neat vinegar to loosen the scale and leave to soak overnight. Then top up with water, and boil and empty two or three times until the smell clears.

3 All the pipework and inner surfaces of washing machines can attract scale, which will in turn encourage detergent residue to stick around. Once a month, run a hot-wash cycle with vinegar in place of your usual detergent, and no clothes.

4 The same applies to your dishwasher. Add a cupful of vinegar to the floor of the machine and then run a hot wash with the machine empty.

5 Use neat vinegar on a soft cloth to wipe down the seals of your dishwasher. Take out the filter and soak it overnight in vinegar to remove the grease. You can also use vinegar in place of your usual rinse aid.

hot! hot! hot!

fridges and freezers

How often do you clean out your fridge and freezer? Let's face it, your fridge is home to all your perishable goods, most of which are just days away from turning from a delicious snack into a science experiment. If you're one of those people who cannot bear to throw food away, and will wait until it's green and moldy, then you need to start paying attention to your fridge.

1 Remove all the food. Try to clean your fridge on the day before you do your weekly shop, when your fridge is at its emptiest. Remove all the shelves and salad drawers – even the door shelves if you can. Wash these in the sink with plenty of hot water and your usual detergent with a cup of white wine vinegar added.

2 Inside the fridge, spray all surfaces with a 50:50 solution of white distilled vinegar and water, and wipe clean with a sponge. Spray any thick residue or deposits, such as fruit juice or milk spillages, with undiluted vinegar and allow to stand for 10 minutes before wiping clean.

3 When you defrost your freezer, use the same process to clean it as you did your fridge. If you have a frost-free freezer, remember to give the insides a wipe down with your vinegar solution every six months.

4 The drain hole at the back of a fridge can get blocked with a nasty looking slime. Not only will this impair the fridge's ability to work properly, it's also pretty revolting to look at. Spray undiluted vinegar above the drain hole and allow it to drip through, clearing the slime as it does.

5 The seals on the insides of the doors of fridges and freezers easily collect dirt and debris. Dip the corner of a soft cloth in neat vinegar, push it into the folds of the seals, then pull it along from one corner to another to pick up crumbs and grime.

6 If you peel a sticker off a new fridge, the tiny residue of glue left behind will attract grease and turn yellow over time. Use neat vinegar on a sponge to remove the stickiness.

7 Have you had some extra smelly cheese in your fridge lately? The smell can linger long after the last crumbs have been eaten. Leave a saucer of neat vinegar in the fridge overnight to clear it.

8 To clean your fridge door, remove everything that is stuck to it and wipe down the door with a 50:50 solution of vinegar and water, and then put back only what you need.

9 To clean and disinfect your trays, soak them in neat white distilled vinegar for a couple of hours, then rinse and leave them to dry naturally.

10 If food has gone off whilst in the fridge, this can leave a nasty smell lingering. To remove the pong, wipe down the shelves with a cloth and neat white distilled vinegar.

11 Remove the grime that builds up on top of the refrigerator using a cloth and neat, white distilled vinegar.

cutting through grease

Where there's food, there's grease and where there's heat, there's burnt-on grease. It's often a stark choice between elbow grease and hours of scrubbing or toxic chemicals that can give off really nasty fumes. Bring on the vinegar and end those kitchen nightmares.

1 If you enjoy a lovely roast dinner, but your heart sinks at the thought of washing down all those burnt-on meat juices, don't fill the meat trays with water and hope for the best. Add a cup of neat distilled vinegar instead, and the grease is guaranteed to shift.

2 Did you leave your saucepan over the heat and forget about it? Scrape as much of the food residue away as you can and then cover with some undiluted white distilled vinegar. Leave overnight and then give it a scrub with a plastic brush. And next time, don't wait for the smell of burning to tell you when dinner's ready – use a timer!

3 We tend to think our microwaves are pretty clean, but they do build up a layer of grease and grime. To remove this, pour a cupful of white distilled vinegar into a glass bowl and heat in the microwave until it starts to boil. Wipe out the microwave with a wet cloth.

4 Cleaning the oven. Isn't that the job we all avoid? Roll up your sleeves and get to it. Mix distilled white wine vinegar with baking soda until you have a fairly sloppy paste. Coat the walls and bottom of your oven and leave the paste to dry. Rinse with clean water and wipe clean. Using this natural paste also avoids the smell you get when you first use the oven after using a chemical cleanser.

5 To keep your hob sparkly and bright, wipe with a 50:50 vinegar and water solution every day. For stubborn food spills, apply neat vinegar and leave for around 10 minutes.

6 If cooker hood filters are removable, soak them in neat vinegar overnight, wash with your usual detergent and then replace. If not, apply the vinegar on a sponge to cut through the grease.

7 To stop smells filtering through the house whilst cooking, boil 1 cup of white distilled vinegar and 2 cups of water in a saucepan at the same time, until all of the liquid has almost disappeared.

8 To remove residue and build-up from your frying pans, boil 2 cups of white distilled vinegar and then rinse clean.

9 When cleaning grill hoods and extractor fans, use a cloth and neat white distilled vinegar to cut through the build up of grease.

10 To make your oven door sparkle and gleam, soak it with neat white distilled vinegar and leave for 30 minutes. Wipe clean using a wet cloth.

cleaning

chef's little ally

While white distilled vinegar is good for cleaning, you can turn to other varieties of vinegar when you don your chef's apron and start to cook. Vinegar really is a gourmet's dream, not only because it has a rich, unique taste, but also because it enhances the flavors and textures of so many other foods.

1 When making pizza sauce, add a generous splash of red wine vinegar – it will intensify the flavor of the tomato and add a pleasing sweetness.

2 Cooking lamb chops? Pour some red wine vinegar over the chops before you grill them to keep the meat tender.

3 Add a few drops of red wine vinegar or raspberry vinegar when stewing fruit to enhance the flavors.

4 When de-glazing a pan after frying meat, use some red wine vinegar. It will pick up all of the residue from the meat and then you can use the sauce to pour over the meat.

5 If you need to de-scale a fish, rub it with vinegar first as it makes the scales lift away more easily. It will also help to remove the fishy smell from your hands.

6 Balsamic vinegar over strawberries has become a bit of a cliché, but it's still delicious. Balsamic vinegar is excellent with lots of fresh and even tinned fruits, such as pears and peaches.

7 You can drizzle balsamic vinegar over a good-quality vanilla ice cream to make an instant dessert.

8 For an easy-to-prepare starter, go for fresh tomatoes and mozzarella sprinkled with basil leaves and balsamic vinegar.

9 If you find that your hands carry a whiffy smell after chopping onions, rub them with white distilled vinegar.

10 When you burn something whilst cooking, the smell can linger on for ages. Pour ½ cup of white distilled vinegar into a bowl and leave it in the centre of the room.

11 To stop doughnuts from soaking up too much grease, try adding a teaspoon of white distilled vinegar to the oil.

chef's cheats

Sometimes vinegar is an essential ingredient when you're cooking; its distinctive flavor is obvious and is a part of the character of the finished food. But there are many occasions when you can use vinegar in your cooking in order to make a real difference to your culinary endeavours. And, best of all, nobody needs to know!

1 Add a spoonful of white wine vinegar to pastry dough to make it extra light and flaky.

2 When cooking pasta, add vinegar to reduce levels of starch and prevent sticking.

3 Add white wine vinegar when making fresh chicken stock as it helps extract the maximum amount of flavor from the bones.

4 When making bread, add a tablespoon of white wine vinegar to help the dough rise. Then brush the loaf with a little white wine vinegar 10 minutes before the end of the cooking time to help the crust develop.

5 When heating canned soups, add a swirl of apple cider vinegar or sherry vinegar just before serving to add zing.

6 If you are using gelatin in a recipe, add a few drops of vinegar to help it set.

7 Add a tablespoon of vinegar to the water when boiling rice to help it fluff up and prevent clumps from forming. If you want to keep cooked rice, sprinkle it with rice vinegar before putting it in the fridge to prevent it from spoiling.

8 We're all guilty of having added too much salt to a recipe, aren't we? No need to panic though, add a teaspoon of white distilled vinegar and some sugar to try to correct the taste.

Did you know that there are often times when vinegar is a cook's secret weapon? You won't taste it in the food, but it will have helped along the way.

9 To stop your cake frosting going sugary, add a drop of white distilled vinegar.

10 Keep moisture in your cakes when baking, by adding a teaspoon of white distilled vinegar to the mix.

11 Keep your cheese fresh and stop it from going moldy by soaking a cloth with white distilled vinegar and wrapping it round the cheese. Then place it in an air tight container in the refrigerator.

12 Soak fish fillets in white distilled vinegar for 30 minutes before cooking. This will help keep them white and also stop them from smelling fishy.

13 To stop sour cream from going off, add a teaspoon of white distilled vinegar to the container. Don't worry, it won't affect the taste and it will keep it fresher for longer.

store cupboard substitutes

We've all been there. You reach that point of no return in a recipe, and then discover that the crucial ingredient you were convinced was in the cupboard isn't actually there. Well, surprising though it may seem, vinegar can stand in for quite a few different ingredients. So, go on, let vinegar be your culinary savior.

1 Although the alcohol in wine is burnt off when it is cooked, some people prefer not to use it anyway. And sometimes you don't want to open a whole bottle when the recipe only calls for a few spoonfuls. For recipes that require a glass or less of wine, you can substitute red or white wine vinegar, or any other vinegar brewed from wine, such as sherry vinegar or even Champagne vinegar.

2 If beer or cider are called for, and you can't lay your hands on either, you can use apple cider vinegar instead.

3 If you don't have a lemon or a lime in the fruit bowl, but you need the juice, just use half the quantity of vinegar.

4 We all know the risks of a diet that's high in sodium. Vinegar doesn't have the same health risks, but is just as effective at enhancing taste. So, if a recipe calls for seasoning, use a few drops of vinegar instead.

5 Buttermilk is a common ingredient in baking. If you don't have any, add a tablespoon of vinegar to a cupful of whole milk, then let it stand for 5 minutes.

6 If you are baking cakes or cookies, and discover that someone used the last of the eggs in the fridge, did you know that you can use vinegar instead? Just use 1 tablespoon of white distilled vinegar plus 1 teaspoon of baking soda to replace each egg in any cake recipe. And, no, your cake won't taste or smell of vinegar.

7 You can make wine vinegar by adding 2 tablespoons of white distilled vinegar to 1 teaspoon of red wine.

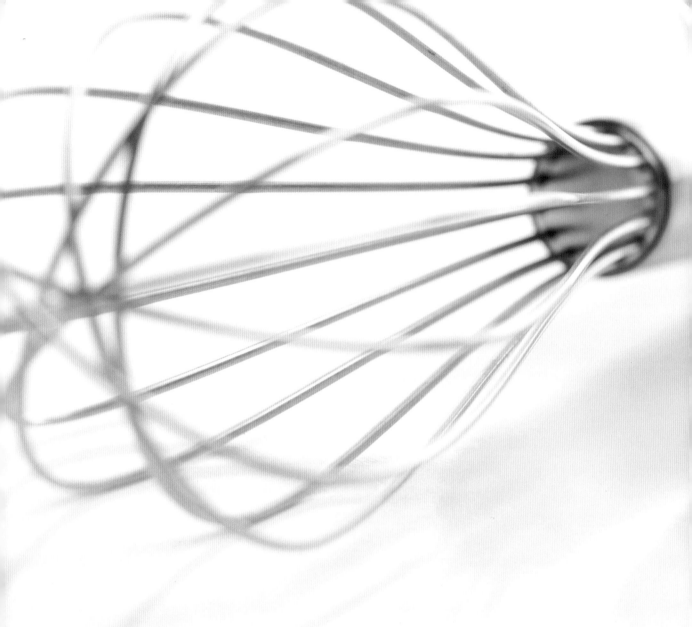

eggs, eggs, eggs!

Not only can vinegar actually replace eggs when baking cakes, it also has a natural affinity with them. It can be called upon when cooking eggs in all their great and various ways, so if your taste is for sunny side up or a stack of morning pancakes, vinegar will be your natural sidekick.

1 When you are boiling eggs, add a splash of vinegar – any type will do, even malt brown vinegar. The vinegar will prevent the whites from leaking if there are any cracks in the shells.

2 If you use the traditional open-pan method of boiling water to poach eggs, add a generous helping of vinegar to the water – it helps prevent the egg whites from spreading out into strands, so the eggs will keep their shape much better.

3 When whipping egg whites to make meringue, add vinegar as you start to beat – the acid in the vinegar helps prevent lumps from forming.

4 Add cider vinegar or white wine vinegar to scrambled eggs to really bring out the taste.

5 Add 2 tablespoons of vinegar to the batter when making American-style pancakes to make the fluffiest stack ever.

6 Sprinkle balsamic vinegar over fried eggs – the acid cuts through the grease and the taste is just amazing.

7 Homemade mayonnaise is absolutely delicious and far superior to anything you can get in a jar. Whisk 2 whole eggs in a blender and slowly add 10fl. oz (285ml) of good olive oil as the blender is running. When they have emulsified smoothly, add a tablespoon of white wine vinegar and then add salt and black pepper to taste. Store in a fridge and consume within 24 hours.

8 When whisking egg whites, wipe the inside of the bowl and whisk with a cloth dipped in neat white distilled vinegar. This will fluff them and create better peaks.

enjoy your vegetables

We all know vegetables are good for us, but many of us could do better when it comes to getting our required daily dose. Vinegar can help to make vegetables more palatable, add a little variety and, in some cases, help us get the most benefit from them.

1 When soaking dried beans and other pulses, add a tablespoon of vinegar to the water. It will help break down the cellulose so that they will cook better and be more easily digested.

2 Keep colours fresh when boiling or steaming vegetables by adding a tablespoon of vinegar to the water – cauliflower will stay bright white and broccoli a fresh green.

3 Cabbage is delicious when cooked properly, and very good for you, but no one wants the smell of old school dinners hanging around for days. Add a cup of vinegar to the boiling water and, hey presto, you have cabbage without the stink.

4 Adding acid in the form of a vinaigrette dressing to green leafy vegetables allows us to absorb their calcium content better.

5 Make a quick, easy – and low-fat – coleslaw by finely chopping some white cabbage and covering in a marinade of 2 parts rice wine vinegar to 1 part groundnut oil with a good splash of soy sauce. Let it stand for a couple of hours for the taste to develop.

6 Washing fruit and vegetables in a solution of 1 part vinegar to 3 parts water helps to remove bacteria, traces of pesticides, and insects. Rinse with clean water and allow to dry. Do not do this to soft fruits as they will absorb too much of the vinegar taste.

7 You can make boiled carrots more interesting by glazing them with a knob of butter, balsamic vinegar and some runny honey. Mix all of the ingredients in a serving bowl and then toss the carrots in the glaze.

8 Pour some balsamic vinegar over roasted root vegetables such as carrots, parsnips, baby onions, and fennel bulbs in the last 10 minutes of cooking to really bring out their taste.

9 Boil some green beans, then pan-fry in 3 or 4 tablespoons of balsamic vinegar with a clove of garlic for a few minutes until the vinegar starts to thicken and coat the beans.

10 Cover thinly sliced cucumber, diced tomato and scallions (spring onions) in a mix of 1 part apple cider vinegar to 2 parts olive oil, with a sprinkling of sugar and leave overnight in a bowl for a fresh-tasting salad.

11 When washing lettuce, add a drop of white distilled vinegar and a pinch of salt to the water, this will help to kill germs and also make bugs float to the surface.

Who'd have thought that all those vegetables – even cabbage, cauliflower and sprouts – could taste so delicious. It must be my secret ingredient. Vinegar!

making varieties of vinegar

Some recipes call for specific vinegars, such as tarragon. If you make your own it will cost you a lot less than the premium price you'll pay for specialty vinegars. You can also make as much or as little as you like, and experiment with different varieties. You will never be stuck for a gift idea again.

1 Use white wine or apple cider vinegar as your basic vinegar – the paler colours will allow you to see the ingredients better and won't stain the herbs or fruits themselves.

2 If you are making a fruit vinegar, or one with red peppers, you can choose red wine vinegar – some people feel that it has a fuller taste than white wine vinegar.

3 Add whole dried chillies for a vinegar that really packs a punch – just a few drops will add a kick to any sauce.

4 For fruit vinegars, such as raspberry or strawberry, gently mash the fruit first, pour the vinegar on and leave in sealed jars for a week. Strain and pour into glass bottles.

5 You can use dried or fresh herbs, such as tarragon, thyme, rosemary and mint, to flavor vinegar. For fresh herbs, bruise the leaves, then insert a bunch in a sterilized jar or bottle, pour the vinegar on and leave for a couple of weeks for the flavor to develop. Either leave the herbs in to carry on imparting their flavor or strain the vinegar to remove the discolorerd herbs and insert a sprig of a fresh herb.

6 If you are using dried herbs, fill the container about a third full with the herbs, add the vinegar and leave for a fortnight, but give it a shake every day. Strain the vinegar through a paper coffee filter or muslin cloth, then return to the bottle.

making vinaigrette

Making vinaigrette couldn't be easier. Just remember the crucial ratio of 3 parts oil to 1 part acid (in the form of vinegar), and you're away. Whisk together, then season to taste with salt and freshly ground black pepper, and decide which flavors you fancy. Try adding some of the following:

1 Smoked Paprika
1 teaspoon of mustard, a pinch of paprika and half a clove of garlic.

2 Orange
2 tablespoons of orange juice, 1 teaspoon of orange peel and 1 teaspoon of honey.

3 Honey & Balsamic
1 teaspoon of balsamic vinegar and 1 teaspoon of honey.

4 Mustard & Honey
1 teaspoon of mustard and 1 teaspoon of honey.

5 Basil
2 tablespoons of fresh chopped basil and 1 teaspoon of honey.

6 Oriental
1 teaspoon of honey mustard, 1 teaspoon of sesame oil and 1 tablespoon of rice vinegar.

7 Chilli
1 teaspoon of chillies and 1 teaspoon of honey.

8 Honey & Garlic
1 teaspoon of honey and 1 clove of garlic.

9 Italian
1 teaspoon of finely chopped Italian herbs and 1 teaspoon of balsamic vinegar.

10 Lemon & Lime
1 teaspoon of lemon juice and 1 teaspoon of lime juice.

11 Lemon and Tarragon
1 teaspoon of lemon juice and 1 teaspoon of chopped tarragon.

12 Cream & Honey
1 tablespoon of whipped cream and 1 teaspoon of honey.

13 Maple & Almond
1 tablespoon of maple syrup and 1 teaspoon of crushed almonds.

14 Ginger & Cayenne Pepper
1 teaspoon of grated root ginger and a pinch of cayenne pepper.

15 Saffron & Honey
1 teaspoon of saffron and 1 teaspoon of honey.

16 Cinnamon & Honey
1 teaspoon of Cinnamon and 1 teaspoon of honey.

17 Fresh herbs are a great addition. Other ingredients you can try include finely chopped salad onions and tomatoes.

18 For an Asian variation, use groundnut oil and rice wine vinegar, with soy sauce instead of salt and some grated root ginger or crushed lemongrass.

19 If you're feeling really indulgent, crumble in some blue cheese, this goes especially well with steak.

20 Vinaigrette does not have to be used on salad – try it instead of butter on jacket potatoes or new potatoes, or over grilled meats. It can also be used as a marinade for chicken or vegetables before you grill them.

making sauces and marinades

Vinegar is the base of many sauces. In barbecue sauces, some sort of sugar is essential for the caramelization process which provides the smoky taste that food cooked over hot coals shouldn't be without, while the acidity in vinegar cuts through this to give a savory zing. And, if you include vinegar in a marinade, it will add taste while also tenderizing meat.

1 For a sticky sauce for ribs, mix a fruit jelly such as redcurrant or cranberry with some dark brown sugar, soy sauce and red wine vinegar – this makes for sticky-fingered heaven.

2 For mint sauce, take a bunch of fresh mint leaves, chop finely with kitchen scissors, cover with white wine vinegar, add a spoonful of sugar and leave for half an hour. Perfect with roast lamb.

3 Light a fire for your taste buds with a fresh tomato salsa. Mix equal amounts of balsamic vinegar, brown sugar, olive oil, and lemon juice, then add finely chopped onion, tomato and a fresh red chilli. The longer you leave it, the more it will burn. Great over burgers.

4 Use apple cider vinegar to marinate chicken before you roast it – add a little soft brown sugar, some salt and pepper and any herbs you like.

5 Add some zing to your white sauce by adding 1 teaspoon of white distilled vinegar.

6 If you are serving Chinese-style party food, leave out small bowls of dipping sauce made from apple cider vinegar, sesame oil and a few sesame seeds sprinkled on top.

7 Follow the Italian model by serving fresh crusty bread alongside very good olive oil with a few drops of balsamic vinegar swirled though.

3

health
and beauty

Whether by external application, or by actually drinking it in some form, vinegar can really make us look and feel our very best. If you're looking for that elusive healthy glow, keep a bottle of vinegar in your bathroom cabinet and make it a part of your daily beauty regime. And, while you're at it, add another bottle to your medicine cabinet where it will more than earn its keep.

While all vinegars offer benefits, this is the section in which apple cider vinegar really comes into its own. Many people swear by its health-giving properties. Buy organic varieties for fewer impurities – look out for the 'mother' of vinegar, those telltale strands floating in the vinegar which indicate that the enzymes are present. If the vinegar has been filtered or pasteurized, many of those active ingredients will have been removed. Check out health food stores for supplies, or you can now buy it very easily online.

first aid kit

Since earliest times vinegar has been used for medicinal purposes, and we can still exploit its benefits today.

1 Spray ice-cold vinegar on minor skin burns, for pain relief and to prevent the formation of blisters.

2 Dissolve 1 teaspoon of salt in half a cup of warm apple cider vinegar and apply it to a bruise as a compress.

3 If you want to shift a headache try vinegar. You should apply it on a cold face cloth laid over your forehead and lie still for 20 minutes.

4 Many headaches are caused by swelling of the blood vessels. To reduce the swelling and give you some relief, inhale the steam from a bowl filled with boiling water with a cup of vinegar added.

5 For muscle aches and strains, apply a hot towel dipped in vinegar as a compress for 20 minutes.

6 To cure a hangover, drink a glass of water with a teaspoon of apple cider vinegar added. If you're feeling especially queasy, add some ginger powder to settle your stomach.

7 Bee stings can be sore and itchy. Apply a compress dipped in neat, white distilled vinegar to reduce swelling.

8 To stop hiccups, try drinking a teaspoon of apple cider vinegar. The taste is quite a shock, and if your throat burns, follow up with a large glass of water.

9 If you have a stiff neck, soak a tea towel in a 50:50 solution of apple cider vinegar and warm water. Squeeze the excess water and apply it to the neck area with a towel over the top and leave overnight.

10 If you suffer from repeated nose bleeds, try mixing a solution of 2 teaspoons of apple cider vinegar in a glass of water, drink this 3 times a day. This will promote the natural clotting properties in the blood.

11 Try relieving the symptoms of a skin rash by rubbing the area with apple cider vinegar 3 times a day.

12 To relieve discomfort of sprained foot, try soaking a brown paper bag in apple cider vinegar and wrap it round the foot and leave overnight. This should help reduce the swelling.

13 To reduce the risk of heartburn after meals, drink 1 glass of water containing 1 tablespoon of apple cider vinegar, before eating.

keeping hale and hearty

Many people swear by the efficacy of apple cider vinegar (ACV) as a provider of health-giving properties, often after other medicines and treatments have failed. While the evidence is only anecdotal, and has yet to be proven in any clinical trials, why not give it a go if you are looking for relief from stubborn symptoms, or feel in need of a natural boost?

1 As a daily tonic to improve your general sense of well-being and digestion, try starting the day with a glass of water mixed with a tablespoon of apple cider vinegar.

2 Drinking apple cider vinegar helps to regulate blood sugar levels, which can contribute to long-term gradual weight loss. Drink 2 or 3 teaspoons in a glass of water before a meal.

3 Long-term arthritis sufferers have found that taking 2 or 3 teaspoons of apple cider vinegar in a glass of water gives them relief from chronic pain.

4 For joint pain you can use a two-pronged attack. Drink 2 or 3 teaspoons of apple cider vinegar in a glass of water up to 3 times a day. You can also apply the vinegar topically: mix a few tablespoons in oil and rub it directly into the affected joints.

5 The acid in apple cider vinegar and other vinegars can help the body absorb calcium, so ensuring that you get the maximum benefit from your food, as well as helping to prevent osteoporosis.

6 If you have prominent varicose veins, try rubbing some apple cider vinegar on them, this should help reduce swelling and also relieve pain.

7 To prevent cramps in your legs whilst sleeping, take a teaspoon of apple cider vinegar before going to bed.

8 To help relieve the pain caused by cramps, douse a towel in a 50:50 solution of apple cider vinegar and water and microwave it for 15 seconds. Apply it to the leg with cramp for instant relief.

9 Ear wax build-up and discharge is very common, especially in children. The trick for keeping it at bay is to dilute one teaspoon of apple cider vinegar in a glass of water and drink every day.

10 The acid in vinegar can erode the enamel on your teeth, so make sure you brush your teeth after using vinegar orally.

11 Apple cider vinegar has the health properties of apples themselves, such as betacarotene and pectin which can help regulate appetite and the levels of bacteria in the stomach, in addition to the benefits of the acids and enzymes formed during the fermentation process.

12 To help relieve morning sickness, try drinking a glass of water with 1 tablespoon of apple cider vinegar and 1 teaspoon of honey when you wake up.

snuffles, sneezes and sore throats

We all know there's no cure for the common cold, but when you are suffering from the effects of one, it is tempting to think that scientists should just pull their fingers out and get on with finding one. Why are they dragging their feet? In the meantime, vinegar can help to alleviate many of the symptoms.

1 To relieve the pain of a sore throat, add a tablespoon of apple cider vinegar to a large glass of warm water and gargle. Repeat every few hours.

2 If you have painful ears, soak some cotton balls in a 50:50 solution of white distilled vinegar and boiled and cooled water, and place them in the ears.

3 Nasal congestion is painful and annoying. To help clear the blockage, place a few tablespoons of apple cider vinegar in a pan and warm them. Remove from the heat and place in a bowl, then lean over it to inhale the fumes.

4 As a treatment for blocked sinuses, try drinking a tablespoon of apple cider vinegar in a glass of warm water.

5 For irritating night-time coughs, sprinkle your pillow with apple cider vinegar and you will get a better night's rest.

6 A hot drink before you go to bed helps when you are feeling lousy. Try mixing equal parts apple cider vinegar with runny honey, enough hot water to warm the mixture, plus a little lemon juice to add piquancy.

7 To aid a tickly cough, mix together 1 tablespoon of melted butter, 1 of apple cider vinegar and 1 of sugar and drink.

8 Hay fever affects many people and can really spoil the summer season. If you are a sufferer, take the following remedy daily throughout the hay fever season: 2 teaspoons of honey and 2 teaspoons of apple cider vinegar in a glass of water.

9 Mix one or two teaspoons of apple cider vinegar with the same amount of honey for an effective cough suppressant. You can also add some ground ginger or cayenne pepper if you like the taste, as they can help to reduce inflammation. Sip the mixture as and when you need it.

My throat
is so sore...
how can
vinegar help?

71

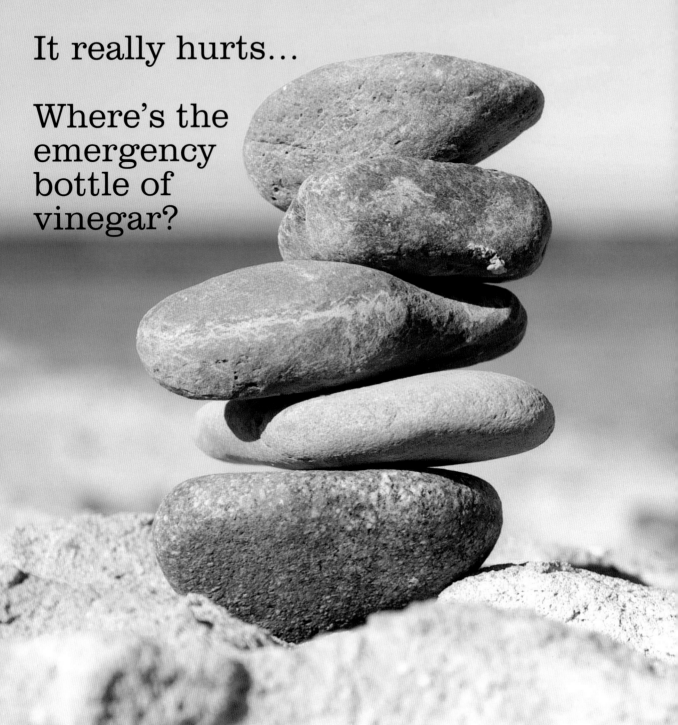

Ouch, I've just been stung by a jellyfish!

It really hurts...

Where's the emergency bottle of vinegar?

vinegar on vacation

We don't like to fear the worst when we go on holiday, but the sun and sea can sometimes cause a few minor problems. Vinegar is a remedy that can easily be sourced – you don't have to track down a pharmacy in a foreign town; you can simply find it in the local supermarket or grocers if you don't have some already in the kitchen cupboard of your holiday home.

1 Dab undiluted white vinegar on to wasp stings and mosquito bites to reduce the pain and stop the infuriating itch.

2 To keep the little pests away in the first place, spray liberal doses of white vinegar around, on surfaces if you are eating outside, and on the skin (avoiding the eyes and any open cuts). The smell is no worse than chemical deterrents and is much better than being bitten.

3 For sunburn, soak a dishtowel in vinegar, place it in the fridge for 20 minutes so that it's cool, and then lay it over the affected area.

4 To settle an upset stomach, which is a common holiday problem, add a tablespoon of vinegar and a tablespoon of honey to a large glass of warm water, and sip slowly.

5 Jellyfish are increasingly common in all coastal waters. If you have been unlucky enough to be stung, you'll know how painful it can be. According to a study published in the Medical Journal of Australia, removing any tentacles and then pouring undiluted vinegar, in any form, over the wound will alleviate pain and prevent the release of more venom – the acid neutralizes the nematocysts. This is not true of stings from the Portuguese Man O'War jellyfish, however. If you've had a run-in with one of those, seek medical attention as soon as possible.

skin deep beauty

Vinegar makes a great skin treatment. It helps to regulate your skin's pH value because of its acidity, and is a natural astringent. Its inherent antibacterial qualities also help to counter the effects of over-production of oil in the sebaceous glands, the classic cause of acne and other unwanted skin eruptions. And all for a fraction of the price of commercial skin care.

1 To relieve itchy skin, either apply a 50:50 solution of apple cider vinegar and water to the affected area on a cotton ball or, for more generalized itching and dry skin, add 2 to 3 cupfuls to your bath water.

2 If you have been chopping garlic or onions, or preparing fish, you can carry the smell around for several days. If you prefer not to smell of yesterday's dinner, wash your hands with white wine vinegar to remove the stink.

3 You can buy over-the-counter treatments for warts, but if you would prefer a natural approach, soak a cotton ball in white distilled or apple cider vinegar, use a sticking plaster to attach it directly to the wart and leave overnight. Repeat this several times until the wart disappears.

4 Age spots can be treated with a mix of 2 parts orange or lemon juice to 1 part apple cider vinegar. Some people substitute onion juice for the fruit juice by blending an onion and then straining the juice. This mix can cause irritation, however, so only apply to the spots themselves.

5 Make a face mask to help reduce open pores by mixing a teaspoon of apple cider vinegar with the whites of 2 eggs. Whisk together and apply to clean skin, avoiding the eye area. Leave for 10 minutes, and then wash off.

6 Make your own toner using a 50:50 solution of white distilled vinegar and water. Apply to the skin daily after cleansing, using cotton wool.

7 To lighten freckles on the body (not the face) rub them with neat, white distilled vinegar.

8 To strengthen your nails and make nail polish last longer, wipe your finger nails with a cotton ball doused in white distilled vinegar, before applying nail polish.

9 Instead of using expensive aftershaves, try using neat, white distilled vinegar as an aftershave lotion.

10 If you suffer from cold sores, apply neat, white distilled vinegar repeatedly throughout the life of the cold sore. This will help it to dry up and also prevent more appearing by killing the bacteria present around it.

11 You can use white distilled vinegar instead of deodorant for underarms. This is a natural alternative that will help neutralise odours.

12 Zap spots as soon as you see the first signs with 1 part apple cider vinegar mixed with 4 parts water. You can gradually try stronger solutions, but try this weaker mix first to see how your skin reacts.

13 For a cleansing daily face wash, mix 1 part apple cider vinegar with 1 part witch hazel and 3 parts boiled and then cooled water.

14 For a full-scale break-out of spots, add a crushed-up aspirin tablet to 1 part apple cider vinegar and 1 part boiled and cooled water. Apply to the affected area, leave for 20 minutes, and then wash off. Repeat daily until the spots dry up.

15 To help relieve aching muscles, add 2 cups of apple cider vinegar to your bath water and soak for 20 minutes.

16 Clean your make-up brushes by dipping them in baby oil and wiping the debris on to a tissue. Then dip them in a cup of white distilled vinegar to remove any leftover residue.

17 Give yourself an at-home facial by adding 3 tablespoons of apple cider vinegar to a steaming bowl of water. Lean over the bowl and cover your head with a towel for a few minutes, allowing the steam to soften and clean the skin.

beauty

your crowning glory

It only takes the occasional bad hair day to make you realise how much of an effect our hair has on how we look and feel about ourselves. Keep your hair in tip-top condition with vinegar treatments and everything else in your life will fall into place. Well, maybe not, but you will have lovely-looking hair.

1 The key to healthy hair is a healthy scalp. Vinegar will relieve itching, dry skin on your scalp and the resultant skin flakes, combating bacteria and adjusting the pH level of your skin. After shampooing as normal, rinse with a cupful of apple cider or white distilled vinegar added to 2 cups of warm water.

2 This vinegar tonic will also help to keep you hair shiny and less prone to tangling, by smoothing the cuticles and helping to remove the build-up of different styling products on the hair shafts, both of which contribute to dull and damaged hair.

3 If you have color-treated hair, you can keep the color true for longer by rinsing with vinegar, rather than by buying expensive specialist shampoos and conditioners.

4 Don't forget your hair brush. The accumulation of grease from your scalp and hair products can result in a pretty revolting layer of grime. Brushes with rubber backs can be scrubbed with an old toothbrush dipped in neat white distilled vinegar. Combs made from a solid piece of plastic can be soaked overnight.

5 Vinegar won't kill the lice, but it can break down the glue that sticks the nits, or egg cases, to the hair shaft. Wash and shampoo the unfortunate child's hair, then pour over a wash of 2 parts water to 1 part white distilled vinegar, making sure none gets in the eyes. Apply lots of conditioner to loosen any tangles and then comb through the hair, section by section. Repeat every 2 to 3 days until all the little visitors have packed their bags and left.

6 When doing an at-home hair dye, add a cup of apple cider vinegar to the final rinse, this will help the colour set.

7 Hair clips and grips can attract grime and grease. The best way to clean them is by soaking them in warm water with 1 tablespoon of white distilled vinegar. Rinse with clean water and allow them to air dry.

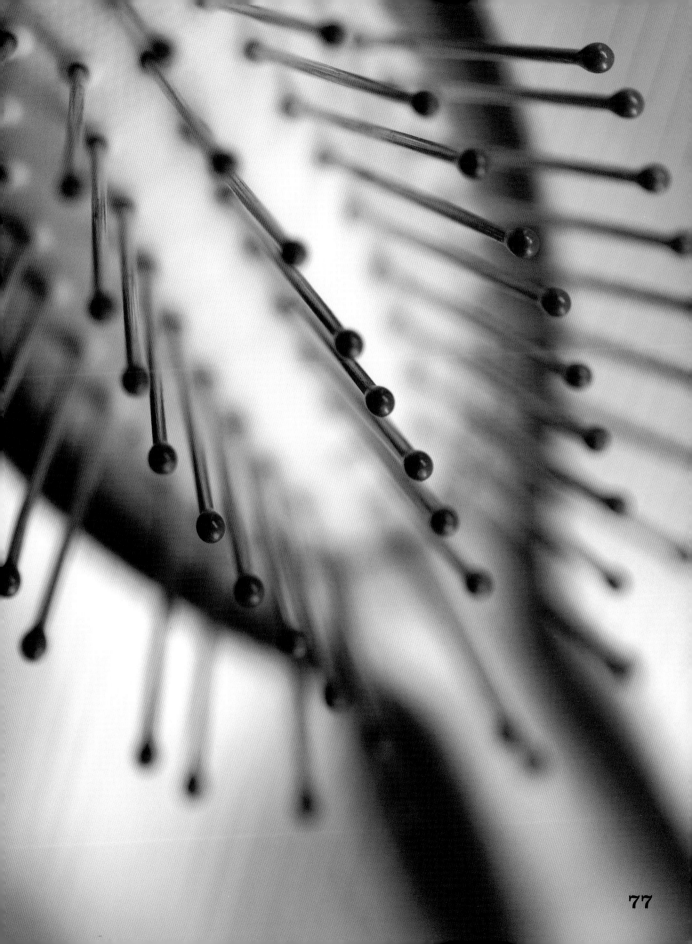

beauty

feet treats

Come the summer months, we all want to have dainty, smooth-skinned toes peeping out of our strappy sandals. But this requires a little work in the build up to the great reveal. Keep your tootsies in tip-top condition by the judicious application of vinegar.

1 Tired, aching and swollen feet? Make a foot spa of warm water, to which you've added a tablespoon of Epsom salts and a cup of apple cider vinegar, and sit back and relax for 20 minutes. The skin on your feet will have softened after its spa treatment, so take the opportunity to remove hard patches using an abrasive foot scraper.

2 Unsightly cracked and dried heels can be treated by wrapping them in a paper towel or soft cloth that has been soaked in apple cider vinegar. Leave for around 20 minutes.

3 For corns and calluses, you can apply apple cider vinegar on a cotton ball overnight, keeping it in place with sticking plasters.

4 Soaking your feet in vinegar can alter the pH value of the skin, which will help to deter athlete's foot. If you do develop it, however, apply undiluted apple cider vinegar on a cotton ball to the affected skin and allow to dry thoroughly before putting on socks and shoes. Repeat daily until the infection clears.

5 Fungal toe nail infections are unsightly. Don't just cover them up with nail varnish, get to the root of the problem. Soak the affected toes in undiluted white distilled vinegar for 20 minutes each day.

6 Feet encased in socks and shoes all day long are a breeding ground for bacteria, which is what will cause that whiff when you remove your shoes. Treat your feet by soaking them in equal parts warm water and apple cider vinegar to keep them fresh and pong-free.

How can I go out to that cool party with my feet looking like this – the heels are all cracked and dry?

Quick, go and grab my vinegar!

4 pets and animals

Our pets deserve the same consideration as us. If you don't like exposing you and your family to unnecessary levels of chemicals, it stands to reason that you want to extend the same care to your pets. But you have to keep up the hygiene levels! Bleach kills germs but can be an irritant, and it is a bit worrying when animals lick or chew their cages. Vinegar is antibacterial and so gives a thorough clean, but won't harm your precious charges – how's that for peace of mind?

You can buy apple cider vinegar for animals from pet supply companies. It is sold to farmers both as a drenching liquid for cattle, pigs and goats, and as a food supplement. You don't have to buy separate supplies, however. Use your own apple cider vinegar as an animal food supplement and ordinary white distilled vinegar for cleaning jobs.

pampered pooches and feline friends

So are you a cat or dog person? Man's best friend or stupid mutt? Spiteful, scratching beast or sphinx-like beauty? Whichever side of the fence you sit on – or perhaps you embrace both equally, and have cats and dogs living with you in perfect harmony – vinegar can help you give your beloved pets the very best of care.

1 For a natural flea prevention regime for dogs and cats, add a few drops of vinegar to their drinking water.

2 Cats are naturally superior and like to maintain that position by finding a high perch. Deter cats from sitting on kitchen and food preparation surfaces by spraying these areas with neat vinegar and allowing it to dry.

3 Clean out a cat's litter tray with a 50:50 solution of white vinegar and water to kill germs and prevent a lingering odor.

4 Wash pet bedding in the washing machine on its own, and add a cupful of vinegar to the final rinse for a really thorough clean.

5 Rigid plastic molded pet beds can be wiped out with a spray of diluted vinegar, but make sure you wipe out with clean water afterwards.

6 Rinse a cat or dog's fur with vinegar after shampooing to make sure that all the shampoo is cleaned out, to add shine and to deter fleas.

7 Wash and disinfect chew toys with a dilute solution of water and vinegar.

8 Clean out a dog's ears with a cotton ball dipped in a solution of half vinegar and half water to clean the bacteria that can lead to infections.

9 Keep your pet's brush clean by soaking it in apple cider vinegar and then rinsing it with cold water.

10 To give your cat or dog a shinier and cleaner coat, add a teaspoon of apple cider vinegar to their drinking water.

11 To discourage your dog from sitting on worktops or other surfaces, spray with neat white distilled vinegar after cleaning.

12 If your pet keeps marking its territory in an unwanted part of the house or garden, spray the affected area with white distilled vinegar.

puppy training

Having a puppy is like having a baby – the sleepless nights broken by heart-rending cries, the need to feed every few hours, the chewed-up furniture. Well, maybe not the last one, but you get the picture. Let vinegar help with all the practicalities and it will make that crucial puppy-training period as painless as possible. Just remember who's in charge.

1 Accidents will happen – usually several times a day for the first few weeks. On hard floors, blot up urine and mop with plenty of hot water with a cup of vinegar added.

2 To deter return visits to the same area, spray with a 50:50 solution of vinegar and water, and allow to dry. It will help to clear the smell as well.

3 Try to keep puppies contained to areas with hard floors if possible. But if they do leave an unwelcome deposit on your carpet, wash with a mix of white distilled vinegar and water, then sprinkle with baking soda. Leave to dry and then vacuum the area.

4 Just as with human babies – everything goes into a puppy's mouth. To put them off chewing the legs of your furniture, spray with some neat white vinegar.

Oh dear! My puppy is so cute, but he keeps leaving little puddles everywhere.

5 When training your puppy to walk with a leash (lead), you'll often find that they are more interested in chewing it. Soak the half that attaches to the collar in neat vinegar and it will put them off.

6 Puppies love chewing shoes, even when you are wearing them. If this is becoming a problem, spray your shoes with vinegar to deter any unwelcome chewing.

7 Young dogs can wreak havoc on well-tended gardens. If they are digging where they shouldn't, spray vinegar on the soil. Don't be tempted to spray vinegar directly on plants, though, or it will kill them.

pet hygiene

those creature comforts

Cats and dogs might not be your thing, or you may just not have enough room for them. If so, there are a whole host of other small animals that you can keep as pets in your home or garden. And vinegar is versatile enough to have applications for the ever-increasing variety of animals we adopt into our lives.

86 pets and an

1 Rats, mice, gerbils, hamsters, dagus and guinea pigs are all popular pets. But having rodents share your home can result in an assault on the nose. Clean out cages regularly with a 50:50 vinegar and water solution to stop your house smelling unpleasant.

2 Clean out cages for tame birds such as parrots, budgerigars, and cockatoos in the same way.

3 Add a few drops of vinegar every time you fill an animal's water bottle to prevent mildew. This is especially useful for bottles on outdoor cages, as sunlight will increase the build-up of mildew.

4 If you keep horses, add a cupful of vinegar to a bucket of water for a final brush in order to give them a really shiny coat.

5 You can also add half a cup of apple cider vinegar to horse feed to deter pesky flies – the bane of a horse's life, especially in the hot summer months.

6 Keeping chickens in the backyard is becoming a popular pastime as we try to become more self-sufficient. Vinegar makes a good cleaner for water bowls, and adding some to the drinking water is said to stop the hens pecking each other as much.

7 A stubborn ring can develop around a fishbowl – it's a combination of scale from the water and food deposits. Scrub with neat vinegar and then rinse well.

8 If you like to encourage wild birds into your garden with bird feeders or a birdbath, keep them clean with vinegar instead of harsh chemical cleaners.

9 Rabbit litter trays can get lined with a limescale-like calcium residue from their urine, which is almost impossible to shift once it has dried on. Soak in undiluted white distilled vinegar and scrub with a hard brush for best results.

10 If they don't have a litter tray, rabbits often choose a corner of the hutch to use as a toilet. The wood can get stained and smelly. Soak with undiluted vinegar for 20 minutes, and then scrub out with plenty of clean water.

wasps, flies and other uninvited guests

Now we might love our pets, but there are other creatures out there who aren't so welcome, and certainly aren't members of the family. Most of them are of the small, scuttling, multi-legged or flying variety. This is where vinegar comes into it's own – use its distinctive smell as a deterrent and its acid nature as a bug killer when necessary.

1 Fruit flies are tiny but very annoying. To keep them away, wash the fruit bowl and the fruit itself in a solution of two-thirds water to one-third vinegar.

2 Keep a spray bottle of undiluted white vinegar on hand to zap houseflies in the kitchen.

3 Make your own wasp traps. Fill a jam jar with vinegar and honey and a little dish-washing detergent. Make holes in the lid and screw it on. Wasps are attracted by the honey and can't get out again, so are killed by the vinegar and soap. Make the hole small enough so that you don't attract bees. Bees are our friends.

4 If you are unlucky enough to share your living space with cockroaches, you will know how tough they are. Douse them in neat vinegar to kill them.

5 Acetic acid is a common ingredient in bed-bug killers. It must come into direct contact with the bugs to do its job, though.

6 When camping, spray the outside of the tent with vinegar to repel mosquitoes, flies and other annoying insects.

7 Kill mealy bugs on plants by applying vinegar directly with a cotton bud. Avoid splashing the plants themselves.

ant attack

Do you have a trail of moving black specks criss-crossing your kitchen?

1 Spray countertops with neat vinegar and allow it to dry in order to deter ants.

2 Stop ants from getting into the house in the first place. Spray a thick line of neat vinegar across doorways to prevent access and kill them off. Do not remove the dead ants – they serve as a further deterrent to other ants. Repeat at least once a week in the summer months, more often if it rains.

3 If you find an anthill in your garden, pour in some neat vinegar followed by boiling water.

4 Make your own bug spray using 2 tablespoons of white distilled vinegar, 2 tablespoons of liquid detergent and 1 cup of water. Add the ingredients to a spray bottle and shake vigorously before using it to zap unwanted bugs.

tangled web

Come the autumn months does your house fill up with eight-legged creatures? Do you have a phobia about spiders? Rather than killing them, try prevention rather than cure, and use vinegar to keep them away instead.

1 Keep spiders at bay by spraying vinegar in the crevices, such as windowsills and corners, where they like to lurk and set their traps. They will be put off by the smell.

Yikes, there is a huge, hairy spider in my bath. Get rid of it!

5

outdoors

Vinegar is not just useful indoors; you can take it outdoors with you too. You can use it for many jobs around the exterior of the house and in the garden, where it is just as effective at tackling tricky jobs as it is indoors. And when it comes to cleaning your car, it makes light work of a task everyone loves to put off, and gives super shiny results.

Are you a keen gardener? Do you look at the rows of different chemicals at garden centers and then shudder? There seem to be so many toxic chemicals available as herbicides, insecticides and soil conditioners. But to many people it just seems wrong to be embracing nature and encouraging plants and wildlife in their own little green patch, only to be introducing noxious chemicals into the ecosystem. So, it's not surprising that organic gardening appeals to more and more people as a concept. Vinegar is an all-natural substance, and can take the place of many of those unappealing concoctions.

in the yard

Take a stroll around the outside of your home and you will soon spot many small maintenance jobs that can be sorted out with the judicious application of some vinegar. Keeping your home running smoothly and causing no harm to the environment while you do it – what could be more satisfying?

1 Keep drains running freely and avoid unwelcome smells in hot weather by applying several cups of undiluted white distilled vinegar, a cupful of baking soda and boiling water in succession.

2 To remove mildew and bacteria build-up on air conditioning units, clean the filters by soaking them in a solution of 50:50 vinegar and hot water for 20 minutes, then scrubbing with an old toothbrush. Wipe over the casing of the air conditioning unit with the same solution.

3 If limescale deposits are accumulating on your outdoor tap, wrap a cloth soaked in undiluted vinegar around it overnight, then scrub with a brush.

4 Pressure hose cleaners are enormously useful for all sorts of work around your garden, but, like any tool that uses a cold water supply, they can develop mildew. Run a cup of undiluted vinegar through the pipes on a regular basis to keep them clear.

5 Hot tubs are very popular, but can play host to harmful bacteria. Every few months empty the tub and wash out with plenty of undiluted vinegar to kill them off. Leave the vinegar to dry before filling the tub again.

6 Paddling pools and other blow-up plastic garden toys can develop mildew if they were not completely dry before they were put away for the winter. If that's the case, wash them down with a solution of equal parts water and vinegar. If stains persist, spray them with neat vinegar and leave for a couple of hours before scrubbing with a soft brush.

7 Wipe down climbing frames and other outdoor apparatus using a 50:50 solution of white distilled vinegar and water.

general

surfaces

One of the most important tasks in the upkeep of our outdoor space is keeping the surfaces in good condition, so that they both look good and are safe to use. Vinegar can be used on a wide variety of hard-landscaping surfaces.

1 Remove unwanted grass, moss, and weeds on paths and driveways by spraying with undiluted white wine vinegar.

2 Wooden decking can get slippery if you allow moss to build up so keep it clear with regular scrubbing using a hard-bristled brush and undiluted vinegar. Allow the vinegar to dry on the wood to prevent a further build-up. If you are expecting a frost, the vinegar will also help stop your decking turning into your own personal ice rink.

3 Garage floors can collect all sorts of grime and muck, such as the oil from car maintenance. Sweep out any loose debris, then mop out with a bucket of hot water with two or three cups of vinegar added to cut through the grease.

4 To keep calcium at bay on bricks, spray with a solution of 50:50 water and white distilled vinegar.

pest control

We all like to attract wildlife to the garden – but only the good guys. Keep unwelcome visitors at bay by using vinegar as a deterrent.

1 Clean out your garbage bins with hot water and a few cups of vinegar, then spray the outside and lid with undiluted vinegar to keep foxes and other scavengers away.

2 Water butts are invaluable in the garden, but can attract mosquitoes. Spray the lid and top with undiluted vinegar to reduce their numbers.

3 If your children have a sandbox, you know how appealing it can be to all the local cats. Pour undiluted vinegar all around the perimeter to put them off. This will also deter ants from creating an anthill in the sand.

4 If you find your compost bins are attracting rats and mice, make sure you aren't including any meat or uncooked food, and spray the bottom edge with undiluted vinegar as a further precaution.

5 Keep ants at bay by pouring white distilled vinegar on the area. This will deter them and keep them from coming back.

6 If you're holding a garden party, keep insects at bay and away from your guests by placing a bowl filled with apple cider vinegar outside.

cars home valet

An automatic car wash is okay for a basic clean, but it is never that thorough. You can pay for a team of eager young men and women at the local garage to do the job by hand, but you can do a better – and cheaper – job at home yourself, and vinegar can guarantee you gleaming results.

1 Adding a few cupfuls of vinegar to your soapy water will increase the shine on the paintwork.

2 Pay special attention to the chrome on the wheels or bumpers. After washing the rest of the car, buff with a soft cloth to which you've added some white distilled vinegar.

3 In icy conditions, wiping over the car windows with a solution of 3 parts vinegar to 1 part water and allowing it to dry will help prevent ice formation, so saving you all that tedious and finger-numbing scraping in the morning.

4 If you've changed your mind about a bumper sticker and want to remove it, you can get rid of any glue residue by scrubbing with neat vinegar.

5 Salt and water deposits thrown up by winter roads can really damage your car if left to dry. Clean off the undersides and around the wheel arches with a bucket of warm water to which you've added 2 cups of white vinegar.

6 If someone has been sick in the car, the smell can hang around for ages. Leave a saucer of vinegar in the car overnight to freshen the atmosphere. Spray any affected upholstery with a solution of 50:50 vinegar and water, and leave to dry.

7 You have to pick the right day to clean your car, as soapy water dries on the paintwork and leaves deposits. To avoid this, add 3 to 4 cupfuls of vinegar to a bucket of clean water and sponge down generously.

8 Wipe the road dirt from your wipers using a cloth and neat white distilled vinegar.

9 Mix a 50:50 solution of water and white distilled vinegar to wipe down your upholstery. Leave it to air dry, you'll be surprised how much the vinegar will neutralise the smells in your car.

10 To make your windscreen sparkle, spray with white distilled vinegar and wipe clean with a damp cloth.

11 To get rid of dirt and stains from car carpets, use a 50:50 solution of water and white distilled vinegar, blot using a cloth and leave to air dry.

12 If you have leather upholstery, clean it using hot, white distilled vinegar and rinse with warm, soapy water.

13 If you have chewing gum or a sticky sweet stuck to your car carpet, soak it with white distilled vinegar to loosen it.

natural vinegar treatments

If you are concerned about the chemicals you use around the home, it stands to reason you will want to avoid the often even nastier liquids that are available to the gardener. Even if you aren't a fully paid up organic convert, try out vinegar to take the place of at least some of those nasty concoctions – and at a fraction of the price.

1 Spray full-strength vinegar on weeds to kill them. Avoid contact with other plants, though. Tough cookies such as poison ivy or ground elder will need repeated applications.

2 Use cotton balls or tightly rolled wads of newspaper soaked in vinegar to keep cats, wild rabbits and other pests away form your flower borders or vegetables patches.

3 To stop slugs and snails snacking on your seedlings, spray them directly with neat vinegar, but avoid the plants.

4 Clean greenhouse windows and the glass in cold frames with a 50:50 solution of water and vinegar to prevent mildew building up.

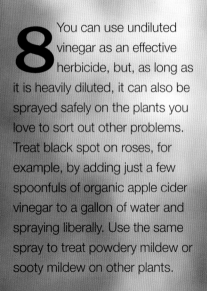

8 You can use undiluted vinegar as an effective herbicide, but, as long as it is heavily diluted, it can also be sprayed safely on the plants you love to sort out other problems. Treat black spot on roses, for example, by adding just a few spoonfuls of organic apple cider vinegar to a gallon of water and spraying liberally. Use the same spray to treat powdery mildew or sooty mildew on other plants.

5 Ornamental terracotta pots can develop unsightly white marks as salts leach out of them. Scrub the pots with neat vinegar to get rid of these.

6 Pumps for outdoor water features and fountains can stop working properly after a while as scale builds up. Remove the pump and run it for 20 minutes in a large bucket of half clean water, half vinegar, recycling the solution as necessary.

7 Use vinegar as a soil treatment around azaleas and other acid-loving plants. Add a cupful of vinegar per 2-gallon watering can. If you use it around your hydrangeas, it will help keep them blue.

9 To clean bird droppings in your garden, spray the area with neat apple cider vinegar and leave to soak for a few minutes, then wipe away clean.

10 When gardening, use neat white distilled vinegar as an antibacterial spray. This will also help remove any stains caused from berries and pollen.

11 If your terracotta pots have fallen victim to mold and mildew, soak them in a solution of 1 cup of white distilled vinegar, a cup of chlorine bleach and 4 litres of hot water. Allow them to soak and then scrub them using a scourer.

Keen gardeners need to be reminded sometimes to take a break from tending the plants and enjoy the spoils of their work. After all, the garden is your outdoor room. So, set up an inviting corner with a table and chairs, or perhaps a bench, and then use vinegar to keep them in tip-top condition.

garden furniture

1 Wipe down plastic tables and chairs with a squirt of dish-washing detergent and a cup of vinegar added to a bucket of water to clean stains.

2 For peace of mind when using outdoor dining tables, spray with undiluted vinegar and then wash down with clean water. The antibacterial effects will make sure all germs are killed.

3 Wooden furniture, such as benches, which is left out all year round can develop an unappealing patina of mildew, water deposits, sap from trees and even bird mess. Scrub in neat vinegar with a hard-bristled brush and leave to dry.

4 Cane furniture that is starting to give can be tightened up by soaking with a 50:50 water and vinegar solution, and leaving to dry in the sun.

5 Fabric-covered cushions can soften hard seats, but it only takes a brief rain shower or some heavy dew for them to get damp and then the chances are that mildew will appear. Scrub with a solution of half water, half vinegar and leave to dry.

6 The same treatment can be used for stains on canvas deck chair covers. Wipe down the wooden frame while you are at it to keep the whole thing looking lovely.

7 To clean the barbeque, spray the grill with undiluted vinegar and leave it overnight. The grease will shift much more easily the next day – just use plenty of hot water. Soak the business end of barbecue tools in undiluted vinegar to get them sparkling again.

8 Keep outdoor umbrellas fresh and free from mildew by using a solution of 1 cup of white distilled vinegar, 1 cup of liquid detergent and warm soapy water. Wipe clean using a cloth and use an old toothbrush to scrub the hard to reach areas.

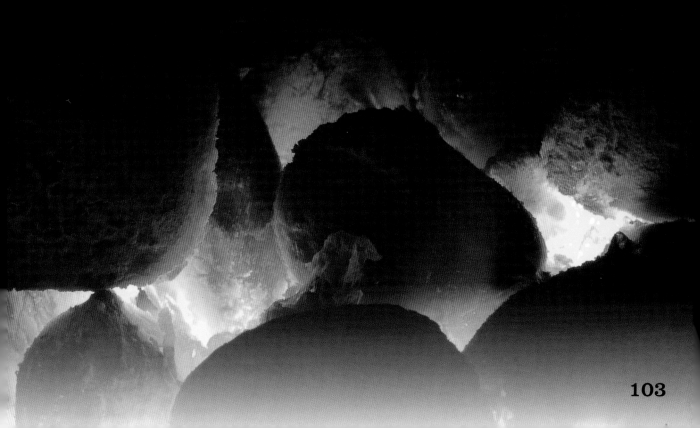

in the shed

Ah, the powerhouse of the keen gardener. But all that green-fingered magic can only happen with decent equipment, so make it a habit to maintain your tools. When it comes to propagating and tending plants, good hygiene is important, and antibacterial vinegar can do half the work for you by killing the germs that can cause problems, and by keeping metal tools and blades in optimum condition.

1 Clean rusty tools by soaking in undiluted white vinegar and then cleaning with sandpaper. Wipe clean with a cloth dipped in lubricating oil.

2 Carefully wipe the blades of your lawn mower with a cloth dipped in neat white vinegar to remove all grass and plant debris.

3 When using hand pruners (secateurs) and pruning shears, you can cause cross infection. Vinegar will kill the bacteria that can spread disease from plant to plant, so use it to clean the blades after every pruning session.

4 Sprinkler heads on garden hoses and watering cans can get blocked with scale. Soak overnight in undiluted vinegar and then poke the holes clear with a wooden toothpick.

5 Sprinkle a mix of equal parts water and vinegar on to a wooden potting shed floor, and then sweep out with a hard broom to clear dust and debris and discourage mildew.

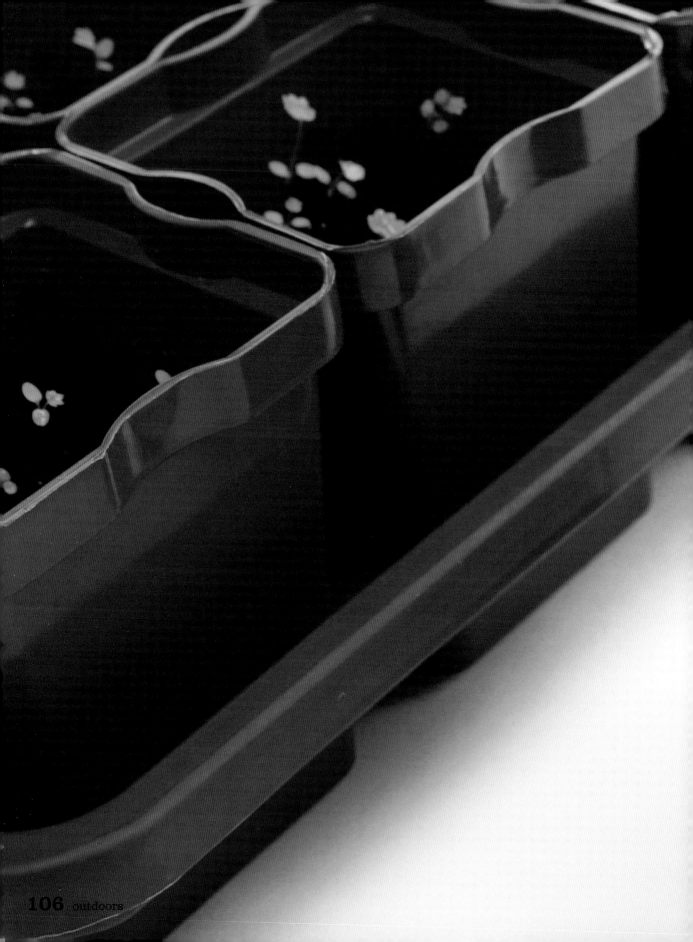

seeds of change

1 Nothing beats the magic of seeing a rash of tiny seedlings appear in pots and trays. But soil-borne fungi can make them suddenly shrivel and keel over. To avoid this, clean out all pots and seed trays with a 50:50 solution of vinegar and hot water before you sow.

2 Some seeds have a hard outer coating which needs to be softened before the seeds will germinate. Soak them overnight in a mixture of one-third vinegar to two-thirds water.

3 If you are using a propagator, whether an electric one or a basic clear plastic cover, clean this in the same way.

6
extra hints and tips

While the kitchen is an obvious home for vinegar, and the bathroom a natural one, you can also find all sorts of other uses for vinegar around your home. Want to spruce up your clothes? Vinegar can help. Doing a spot of redecoration? Yes, it can help with that too. Along with cleaning your jewellery, helping cut-flowers last longer and even cleaning your computer.

If you have a family, you start to think even more deeply about what cleaning products you use. We want to avoid harsh chemicals, while maintaining a reasonable level of cleanliness. We are also warned not to create too clean an environment. This is because our children won't build up any resistance to everyday dirt and low-level bacteria, and will be more likely to develop asthma and other allergies. Roll out the vinegar for cleaning around kids, and strike a happy balance in your home.

DIY and decorating

One of the secrets to great results when you are doing any sort of renovation around the home is thorough preparation. It's always tempting to skip straight to the more enjoyable bit, such as the painting, but you know it won't turn out well if you skimp on the groundwork. So, let vinegar help you to do a better job.

1 When tiling it's important to clean the excess grout off the faces of the tiles, as it's almost impossible to remove once it has set solid. Use a 50:50 mix of white distilled vinegar and water to cut through the grout.

2 Slow down drying time when you are plastering small patches by adding a tablespoon of vinegar to the plaster. This will give you a better chance of achieving a smooth finish.

3 Old paintbrushes can set solid. If you want to restore suppleness to the bristles, soak them in white distilled vinegar overnight. If they are still stiff, warm the vinegar gently and simmer for approximately 20 minutes in a pan on the hob.

4 Vinegar is great when you are stripping wallpaper because it dissolves old wallpaper paste. Spray on generous amounts of a mix of 50:50 water and vinegar, giving it a few minutes to soak in and do its work before you start to scrape.

5 Use the same process for removing any excess or dried-on glue in household projects.

6 When you clean down woodwork before painting, add several cupfuls of vinegar to your bucket of water – it will help remove the grease that stops the new paint adhering properly.

7 Rust on tools or nails and screws can be removed by soaking in undiluted white distilled vinegar.

8 Clear mildew and lichen from outdoor walls before painting by scrubbing with undiluted vinegar on a hard brush, then washing with clean water.

9 To clear paint smells in a room more quickly, leave an open bowl of vinegar on a shelf.

10 When decorating, it's inevitable you will splash some paint on the window. To remove it safely, dab some hot, neat white distilled vinegar on it and leave it to soak in, and then scrape it gently using a thin bladed tool or toothbrush.

11 Make your own woodstain by mixing white distilled vinegar with water-based ink and apply to the wood using a brush or cloth.

12 To remove from woodwork stubborn white ring stains that have been left by wet cups and glasses, rub with a 50:50 solution of white distilled vinegar and olive oil.

13 Keep your hands from drying out when using plaster by washing your hands with normal soap and then rinsing with a 50:50 solution of white distilled vinegar and water.

14 Before painting walls, clean the surface with a solution of 1 part white distilled vinegar to 4 parts water. Wipe down using a cloth and leave to air dry before applying paint.

wardrobe makeovers

Are you always immaculately turned out or do you look slightly grubby around the edges? If it's the latter, it might be time to have a long, hard look through the clothes and shoes in your wardrobe, and see how vinegar can help spruce them up.

1 Salt water marks on shoes are a common hazard during the winter. You can get rid of them by spraying on a mix of equal parts water and vinegar, and rubbing with a soft clean cloth.

2 Keep shoe and boot leather in good condition by applying a mix of linseed oil and vinegar. Apply with a cloth, then buff to a shine with a second clean cloth.

3 To fluff up woollen jumpers and restore softness, add 2 cups of vinegar to the final wash cycle.

4 Woollen jumpers can carry perspiration smells even after washing. To avoid this, spray the underarms of your sweaters with a spritz of 1 part vinegar to 2 parts water before washing.

5 Moths seem to be a hazard that never go away. You can deter them by soaking cotton balls in vinegar, placing them in plastic bags pierced with a few holes and hanging the bag from the hook of a coat hanger in your wardrobe. The smell will put off the moths.

6 When you let down a hem, say on a pair of trousers a child has grown too tall for, the old stitching can be visible. Apply vinegar on a cotton ball on the wrong side of the fabric, spray with water and iron to close up the holes.

7 To deal with the perennial problem of smelly trainers, soak old tea bags in vinegar and leave them in your shoes overnight.

8 To keep your swimming costume smelling fresh and looking vibrant, soak in a solution of 50:50 white distilled vinegar and water, then rinse and leave to dry naturally.

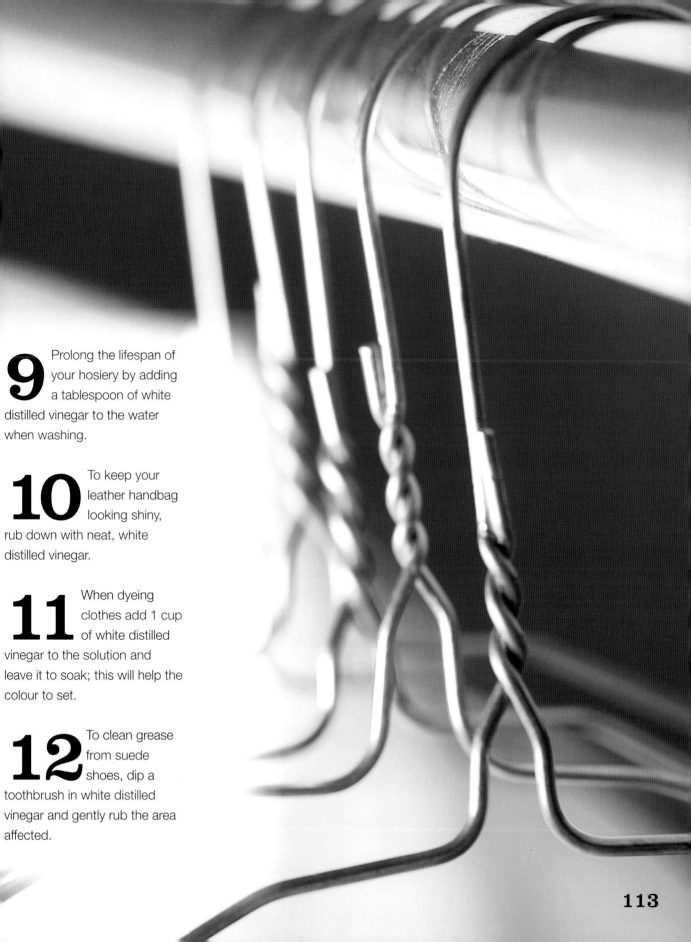

9 Prolong the lifespan of your hosiery by adding a tablespoon of white distilled vinegar to the water when washing.

10 To keep your leather handbag looking shiny, rub down with neat, white distilled vinegar.

11 When dyeing clothes add 1 cup of white distilled vinegar to the solution and leave it to soak; this will help the colour to set.

12 To clean grease from suede shoes, dip a toothbrush in white distilled vinegar and gently rub the area affected.

babies and young children

Vinegar is the perfect cleaning agent to use around young children. It's antibacterial, so you don't need to worry about germs, but using it will not expose your precious bundles of joy to harsh chemicals that can cause skin reactions or trigger allergies.

1 Just as soon as they are old enough to reach out and grab, everything goes in babies' mouths. You can't be too paranoid about this, but for peace of mind you can periodically wipe down plastic toys with a 50:50 mix of water and vinegar. Do this more often if your child or visiting children have a cold.

2 Bath time wouldn't be the same without toys, but they do seem to attract mildew almost immediately. To prevent that yucky moment when you have to scoop black gunk out of a rubber toy, soak all the toys overnight in a strong vinegar solution, at least 50 per cent, once a week.

3 Baby clothes can retain a sour milky smell, even after washing. Add a cup of white distilled vinegar to your fabric softener dispenser to clear lingering smells.

4 When your baby starts on solid food, their bibs can often carry the signs of a week's worth of meals. Carrot and mashed banana stains are the worst. Soak bibs in a solution of vinegar before washing to get better results.

5 High chair trays – and indeed the seats and every conceivable nook and cranny – get coated in bits of food. Brush out loose crumbs and debris, and then wipe out with neat vinegar on a cloth to really get things clean.

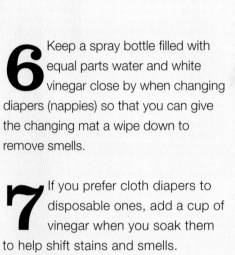

6 Keep a spray bottle filled with equal parts water and white vinegar close by when changing diapers (nappies) so that you can give the changing mat a wipe down to remove smells.

7 If you prefer cloth diapers to disposable ones, add a cup of vinegar when you soak them to help shift stains and smells.

8 Clean baby board books by wiping them with neat white distilled vinegar.

9 To make baby bottles sparkle and gleam, fill with 2 tablespoons of white distilled vinegar and hot water. Then, leave to soak and scrub with a bottle brush.

10 Keep potty training hygienic and fresh smelling, using vinegar. Use a damp cloth and a 50:50 solution of white distilled vinegar and water to wipe the potty.

fun stuff for older kids

Fads for different toys come and go, and a games console seems to be an obligatory fixture in every household with children of a certain age. But the appeal of the chemistry set is enduring. What child wouldn't be thrilled to be given free licence to create fizzes and bangs and transform everyday objects? Create your own experiments at home with some $C_2H_4O_2$ – or humble acetic acid to you and me.

1 This one is best done outdoors! Create a bottle rocket by filling a small plastic water bottle with a couple of inches of vinegar. Twist a large spoonful of baking soda into the middle of a piece of kitchen towel and push it inside the bottle. Loosely screw on the lid and give it a good swirl to mix. Place the bottle upright on the floor and retire to a safe distance to watch the launch.

2 Drop a hard-boiled egg in a glass of vinegar and leave overnight. The acid will react with the calcium carbonate in the shell, releasing bubbles of carbon dioxide, and the shell will soften. Take the egg out of the vinegar and it will absorb carbon from the air and harden again.

3 Or you can take it a stage further and make naked eggs. After the first 24 hours, change the vinegar for fresh vinegar and leave for another 24 hours. The shell will dissolve completely, leaving just the membrane holding the egg together. Handle with care!

4 While we're talking about eggs, you can also dye them in a range of rainbow hues by soaking them in a cup of water to which you've added a tablespoon of white wine vinegar and a few drops of food colouring for 5 to 10 minutes. The vinegar starts to break down the shell and allows the dye to be absorbed more evenly.

5 Amaze and mystify your friends with the knotted chicken bone trick. If you soak a chicken bone in vinegar overnight, it will become soft and rubbery. So what? Well, while it's still pliable, tie it in a knot like a piece of string. Then let it harden again. See if your friends can work out how you did it.

6 This is very cool, but very messy, so work over some plastic sheeting. Make a paste from 6 cups of flour, 2 cups of salt, 2 cups of water and 2 tablespoons of vegetable oil, then form this mixture into a volcano shape around a small upright drinking bottle, avoiding the hole. Fill the bottle with warm water almost to the top and add several drops of dish-washing detergent. Add 2 tablespoons of baking soda, then pour in some vinegar and watch your very own Vesuvius erupt. You can add red food coloring with the water for a fiery, molten effect.

home office

1 Keep CDs and DVDs smear free and less prone to playback error by wiping with a soft clean cloth that has been dipped in white distilled vinegar. Always wipe from the inner ring outwards, never in circles.

2 To clean your computer, first vacuum to remove dust and loose debris, then wipe down the casing, leads, mouse, and keyboard with a soft damp cloth (not wet) sprinkled with some white distilled vinegar. Remember to unplug your computer before you start!

3 Remove sticky residue from your scissors using a cloth that has been dipped in white distilled vinegar.

4 Telephone earpieces collect grease and grime on a daily basis. Dip a cloth in neat, white distilled vinegar and wipe the receiver, once a week.

5 To remove dirt and ink stains from your pen and pencil pot, soak it in warm water, adding 1 tablespoon of white distilled vinegar and 1 teaspoon of baking soda, for 10 minutes. Scrub the insides using a scouring sponge and rinse with clean water.

blind side

1 Vertical slatted blinds are a pig to clean. One of the easiest and most thorough methods is to buy a pair of white cotton gloves specifically for the purpose. Dip your gloved fingers and thumb into a solution of equal parts vinegar and water, and run your hands carefully along each slat, cleaning the top and bottom in one go.

flower power

1 To prolong the life of freshly cut flowers, add a tablespoon of apple cider vinegar and a teaspoon of sugar to the vase water, and replace the fortified water every 2 to 3 days.

2 One reason why flowers wilt is that they are affected by bacteria in the vase. Clean vases thoroughly to get rid of any lurking bacteria and water-line marks by filling with half water and half white wine vinegar and leaving to soak for a few hours.

3 Clean the crusty deposits on flowering houseplant trays by soaking them in undiluted white vinegar.

a mixed bag

And finally…a few other uses for vinegar that you might not have thought of, from keeping your flowers fresh and your jewellery sparkling to giving your computer a good clean and making your smile bright!

1 To whiten teeth and remove stains, wipe over the surface with a cotton ball dipped in undiluted vinegar. Brush your teeth after doing this to prevent the acid in the vinegar continuing to work on your teeth as this can cause damage to the enamel.

2 To clean dentures and kill micro-organisms, soak overnight in a solution of half white distilled vinegar and half water.

3 Clean spectacle and sunglasses lenses by wiping with a soft cloth dipped in white distilled vinegar to keep them smear free.

4 Silver tarnishes over time when exposed to the air as the surface starts to oxidize. To keep your candlesticks and photograph frames looking shiny, clean them with a cup of white distilled vinegar to which you've added a teaspoon of salt and enough flour to make a paste. Apply this paste all over the surface and allow to sit for 20 minutes, before wiping clean with a soft cotton cloth.

5 Use can use the above process for pewter, copper, or brass, so try and keep all your metalwork bright and shiny.

6 Soak silver jewellery in a solution of equal parts white distilled vinegar and baking soda for an hour or two to really get it sparkling, especially the links of silver chains which are tricky to clean.

7 Soak gold jewellery in 1 cup of apple cider vinegar for 15 minutes. Remove it and buff using a dry cloth.

8 To remove chewing gum from clothes or carpets, warm up some white distilled vinegar and apply it to the area affected. Leave it to soak and then gently loosen it.

9 If you have silk flowers around your home, keep them dust-free by spraying them with white distilled vinegar and leave them to air dry.

10 To remove the whiff of a lingering perfume from your body, apply neat, white distilled vinegar to the area.

11 To clean the fireplace and remove grime and soot, mix 1 cup of white distilled vinegar with ½ cup of baking soda. Mix into a paste and apply to the area using a cloth.

12 To remove coffee and tea stains from your best china, use a 50:50 solution of white distilled vinegar and salt. Mix into a paste and apply to the stain. Leave to soak for a few minutes and rinse.

13 Mattresses harbour germs and bacteria. To sanitise your mattress, mix a 50:50 solution of white distilled vinegar and water in a spray bottle. Spray evenly over the mattress and leave to air dry.

14 To clean metal and plastic lamp shades, add 2 tablespoons of white distilled vinegar to warm water and gently wipe using a cloth.

15 When cleaning fabric lamp shades, add 2 tablespoons of white distilled vinegar to warm water and soak a cloth in the solution. Wring the water out of the cloth and gently wipe away the dust and leave to air dry.

16 Curling irons have a habit of collecting grease and grime, which then transfers to your hair. To clean them, ensure they are completely cool, then mix a solution of 1 tablespoon of white distilled vinegar and 1 teaspoon of salt. Form a paste and gently rub it all over in a circular motion. Wipe clean with a damp cloth.

17 Suitcases travel all over the world without a second thought to their cleanliness. Before your next trip, spray them inside and out using a 50:50 solution of white distilled vinegar and water. Wipe clean using a damp cloth. You'll find that your clothes will smell fresher when you unpack.

18 Stickers can be hard to remove or sometimes leave a sticky residue. Soak a corner of a cloth in white distilled vinegar and apply it to the sticker or sticky area and allow the vinegar to soak through before peeling away easily.

19 To clean the grime off white notice boards, add 2 tablespoons of white distilled vinegar and 1 tablespoon of baking soda to water. Using a cloth, wipe the board clean.

20 Ornaments dotted around the home are often forgotten about and yet collect grease and grime every day. When cleaning them add 1 cup of white distilled vinegar to warm water and gently wipe using a cloth.

21 To remove grease and grime that can build up in your flower vases, fill the vase with warm water and two tablespoons of white distilled vinegar. Leave to soak for one hour then rinse.

22 When using an oil burner in the home, add 1 teaspoon of white distilled vinegar to the burning oil. This will help neutralize the smell in your home.

23 Candlewax, when spilt, can be very stubborn to remove. Spray the affected area with neat, white distilled vinegar and leave to soak for a few minutes to loosen it. Then, use a thin bladed tool to gently scrape it away.

24 The rubber rim inside washing machines is renowned for grease build-up. Spray with neat, white distilled vinegar and leave it to soak for 30 minutes. Then add a cup of white distilled vinegar to the machine and run a hot rinse to clear away the debris.

25 To sanitise headphones and remove grease, wipe gently using a cloth dipped in white distilled vinegar.

26 To clean and refresh your child's push chair, spray with a solution of 50:50 white distilled vinegar and water. Then wipe clean using a damp cloth and allow to air dry.

27 Clean the inside of a thermos flask by adding 3 tablespoons of white distilled vinegar and 1 tablespoon of uncooked rice, fill with warm water and shake vigorously. Then empty and rinse using warm water.

28 Don't be afraid of cleaning crystal glasses, with vinegar, there is a simple solution. Add 1 cup of white distilled vinegar to a bowl of warm water. Place the glasses in the bowl and leave them for a few minutes. Remove them and place on a draining board to air dry.

29 Clean storage jars by wiping them with neat, white distilled vinegar.

30 To clean a tea pot, fill with boiling water and add 1 cup of white distilled vinegar. Leave to soak for 30 minutes and then rinse with clean water.

33 Watch straps, leather or plastic, can harbour grease and grime. To clean, add 1 tablespoon of white distilled vinegar to 1 cup of warm water. Using a cloth, gently wipe the straps and fastener.

34 Daily contact with door handles can leave them with fingerprint marks and also full of bacteria and dirt. Mix a 50:50 solution of baking soda and white distilled vinegar. Wipe the solution over the handle using a damp cloth. Repeat every 2 to 3 days.

31 Glass bottles can be easily cleaned using 1 tablespoon of white distilled vinegar and 1 teaspoon of salt. Place the cap on the bottle and shake vigorously. Then rinse with clean water and leave to air dry.

35 To get rid of the musty smell lingering in your gym bag, spray the insides with a 50:50 solution of white distilled vinegar and water. Leave it to air dry.

32 To clean the glass face of watches, mix a 50:50 solution of white distilled vinegar and water. Dip your cloth into the solution and gently wipe the glass in a circular motion.

36 If diesel or petrol has spilt on to your clothes when filling up the car, add 1 cup of white distilled vinegar to the washing machine on the final rinse to clear the smell.

37 House keys are carried round everyday and pick up grease, dirt and bacteria. To clean them, dip a cotton bud in white distilled vinegar and work into the grooves and wipe clean with a damp cloth.

38 To clean glass and plastic clock faces, spray a solution of 50:50 white distilled vinegar and water on to a cloth and wipe clean.

39 Give your child's car seat a thorough clean by spraying all over with a 50:50 solution of white distilled vinegar and water. Wipe the plastic down using a damp cloth, and leave to air dry.

40 Television remote controls can harbor grime and bacteria. Wipe them using a cloth and neat white distilled vinegar.

general

41 The letter box on the front door is often left with fingerprint marks and grease from the road fumes. Wipe clean using a cloth dipped in a 50:50 solution of white distilled vinegar and water.

42 Clean the saddle and handle bars on your bicycle using a solution of 50:50 white distilled vinegar and water. Dampen a cloth with the solution and wipe clean.

43 Bicycle helmets can smell musty from your head sweating whilst cycling. Spray the inside with a solution of 50:50 white distilled vinegar and water and leave to air dry.

44 Your child's favourite teddy bear can harbour bacteria and grime. Spray all over using white distilled vinegar. Then, place inside a pillow case and wash on a normal cycle in your washing machine.

45 Camping is great fun, but tents can easily become weathered over time. Spray the outside and inside with a 50:50 solution of white distilled vinegar and water and wipe clean with a cloth. This will also help keep bugs away.

46 To clean your sleeping bag, add 2 tablespoons of white distilled vinegar to 1 cup of water and use a damp cloth to wipe clean.

47 Plastic and metal fans collect dust and dirt. To clean them, ensure the appliance is switched off and then remove the front grill. Wipe the blades clean with a cloth using neat, white distilled vinegar and leave to air dry.

48 Make your own draw liners to keep clothes fresh by spraying plain paper with neat, white distilled vinegar and place at the bottom of the draw.

49 To keep cigarette ashtrays clean and smelling fresh, soak in a solution of 50:50 white distilled vinegar and water for 30 minutes. Rinse with clean water.

50 To remove dirt from your banisters, wipe them with neat white distilled vinegar and then use a dry cloth to buff them.

51 Plastic clothes pegs are exposed to all kinds of weather and collect dirt easily, which can then transfer onto your clothes. Soak them for 10 minutes in a bowl of warm water and add 2 tablespoons of white distilled vinegar. Rinse with clean water and leave them to air dry.

52 Wipe your washing line clean using a cloth dipped in neat, white distilled vinegar.

53 Keep your hot water bottle from gathering mildew by adding 1 tablespoon of white distilled vinegar when filling it with boiling water.

54 Rubber wellington boots are best cleaned by placing them in a bowl full of warm water and 1 cup of white distilled vinegar. Leave them to soak for 30 minutes and then use a cloth to wipe them.